Dear M

Hope yo

and thanks for joining this
journey with me. Hugs!

The Circles of Life Anna

My Ukrainian Family's Odyssey of Secrets,
Love and Survival from Pre-War Odessa to
the Promised Land and America

Anna Aizic

THE CIRCLES OF LIFE: My Ukrainian Family's Odyssey of Secrets, Love and Survival from Pre-War Odessa to the Promised Land and America

Copyright ©2014 by Anna Aizic
Library of Congress Control Number: 2014940601

ISBN: 978-0-692-22173-0

The author wishes to thank the following websites in which some of her stories, in slightly different form, have already appeared: the JewishGen.org Odessa KehilaLink site, published by Ariel Parkansky, and the Keren Kayemet LeIsrael-Jewish National Fund.

Published by Meir House Press
www.annaaizic.com
Editing: Karen Carter
Tree Image © Kuttelvaserova Stuchelova
Cover and Interior Design: JW Manus

Editor's Note

In her memoir in letters, Anna Aizic manages to transcend numerous potential hazards of the form to engage and enlighten her readers. While she initially put this collection together in order to pay homage to her loved ones and preserve for her children the history of their fascinating family, I believe she has also managed to produce an important historical document. The personal accounts she includes of life during and after World War II in the stunning port city of Odessa, Ukraine, echo with her remarkable extended family's indefatigable hope and humor and, as Anna would say, love of Life. Yet they are mixed with the tragic realities of existence in a Communist system that had no tolerance for Jews who wished to escape its rule. Anna Aizic's memoir follows her family's eventual yet imperfect escape to Israel, the ultimate goal as taught to all by her beloved Zeida in his secret Ulpan of the late 1960s and early 1970s. It also reveals how, despite a penchant for tragedy that seemed to follow her family from Odessa to Israel and even to America—where Anna was eventually diagnosed with, and survived, breast cancer—the seemingly unbearable is somehow overcome due to her family's powerful legacy that includes not only hope and humor, but a willingness to acknowledge, savor and share its many stories.

Karen Carter
Denver

To Meir Davidovich Skulski, my Zeida,
his sons Karl, and (my father) Emil Skulski,
and
for Maria Somoylovna Tikh, my Masha.

INTRODUCTION

Anna Emilyevna Skulskaya, known to family and friends as Anushka, was my name, until unforeseen events changed my life forever.

When I was diagnosed nine years ago with breast cancer, I decided to write letters to my young children, who were then five and eight years of age. Those letters comprise this book. *The Circles of Life* offers glimpses of a journey that brought three generations of my family from Ukraine to Israel and America. It is also a personal account of change, growth, new beginnings, love of Life and hope.

I give endless thanks to my mother, Alla Skulskaya/Berdichevski (known in Israel as Alliya Meir), for her memories, support and love.

Anna Aizic

CONTENTS

Part 1

LETTER ONE: PEARL BY THE SEA

"…and I am going to visit the cobblestone streets of the French Boulevard," my sister announced on the phone from Israel the other day, "…and the acacia trees," she said, "…and the funicular ride down to the Lanzeron beach…and, of course, Odessa!" She sounded angry, even though I never said a word. "And Mom is coming, too."

Was it her casual call that had exposed the raw emotions left between us, after years of barely speaking? Or her planned trip to the land from which we were torn as little girls, forever forbidden to return… let alone visit with our mother?! I couldn't make up my mind what shocked me more, couldn't make any sense out of it…unless this was my sister's way of asking me to come along and join the trip, to close a few circles and start anew, just the three of us?

Her call had evoked a wide range of sensual memories of smells, sights and sounds from the land I used to call Home. Footsteps echo, bouncing from the cobblestone streets of the French Boulevard, leading to the marble stairs down to the hassled, bustling seaport of Odessa, the resort beaches of Arcadia and Lanzeron, with their neat rows of blue chairs and white towels. The polished pebbles of the Black Sea my sister and I used to collect, the gentle breeze of salty mist saturated by the sweet acacia fragrance that, once landed on skin, immediately evaporates, leaving traces of salty circles.

In a photo of Lanzeron Beach, located a few minutes away from the Odessa central street of Deribasovskaya, my mother is in her late twenties, blond and pretty. She is seated on a beach chair, wearing a straw hat and a shy smile. My sister and I sit on the nearby sand, collecting pebbles shining in the bright sun. My father, Emil, as usual is behind the camera.

Shortly after my sister phoned, her chatty monologue started fading until it was replaced by whispers from fuzzy Odessa, just as in a song: "Ex Odessa, Zhemchuzhina u morya." Oh Odessa, the pearl by the sea.

LETTER TWO: TOLCHOK

Born in this eclectic city by the Black Sea, my family often visited places like the Odessa Opera House, a Neoclassical building with statues and gilded fountains. But one day, all that suddenly changed and my family began visiting a place called Tolchok, a bazaar.

In another photo my mother is holding tight to my hand as we cross a busy street with loud vendors selling different goods: This is Tolchok. Tolkuchka, "to shove" in Russian, was the largest marketplace in Ukraine during the 1960s and 1970s.

And Tolchok was the place where my sister and I spent many weekends during the year of 1970, watching our parents sell our beautiful French glass works by Jean Daum and Émile Gallé, our Chinese

Tittot crystal and mahogany sculptures, my mother's gold earrings, my father's antique daggers…and soon, all the pretty things from our two-bedroom apartment in Cheromushki, behind the green lush hills, were gone. They had all vanished, one by one, into the hands of strangers.

Why did this happen?

My father Emil requested a travel visa in 1970. A fairly simple matter, you may say, to leave Russia and go to Israel, right? It is not exactly as simple as today. During the 1970s of the Communist regime, it was considered as both an act of outrage as well as one of courage and madness. Requesting a travel visa from the watchful bulldogs of the Iron Curtain was the same as signing your own execution order; nothing but depravation, harassment and an unforeseen future lay on the horizon.

The outcome was predictable: My family was declared Refusnik, Soviet Jews who were refused a travel visa to leave Russia, and my father was fired from a well paid position as a lead chemical engineer of a Saint Petersburg pharmaceutical corporation.

And that is how, instead of visiting the pretty Odessa Opera House, my family ended up spending weekends in the hassled streets of Tolkuchka, selling all we had just to survive.

We had joined the rest of the Soviet Jews who faced the same destiny: stripped of all possessions, keeping nothing but their pride and love for freedom, facing harassment, ridicule, impoverishment and treated as though we ought to vanish into the Gulags of Siberia.

Tolkuchka was a strange place; you could get anything there. Vendors from the village sold their produce, sharing a corner street with well dressed people and offering anything from a mink Sobel hat to a jar of black caviar or a stick of Medvedeva kielbasa, bear-meat sausage. At the next table a man with gold teeth might sell iron nails, a stuffed armadillo, ivory from Africa and a scroll of silk from India.

My family's possessions fit in well with those surroundings, especially my favorite gift from my father at my ninth birthday. It was a stuffed king cobra (*Ophiophagus hannah*) with a natural predator, mongoose, both of them locked in a fatal position as the mongoose's jaw closed on the snake's twisting body. My mother despised it but I was fascinated by this frozen moment of two creatures at the crux of victory and defeat. That was gone first, followed by antique books, my lacquered French shoes, a silk-laced dress, Mother's jewelry....

Tolkuchka was a place of great adventures for my sister and me. We would feast on fresh strawberries and dried chanterelles (edible mushrooms), baked goods and exotic fruits from the Near East such as bananas and oranges that were sold by bearded Georgian vendors right from their brown leather suitcases. And at the end of the day at Tolkuchka, my father would always treat us to a cup of chilled Kvass, a dark sour Russian beer, a national drink made from fermented rye or barley.

LETTER THREE: CHEROMUSHKI

"Are you planning to visit Cheromushki, too?" I asked my sister during her phone call, embarrassed for not being attentive and hopeful she had not noticed. But her chatty voice convinced me she was oblivious to my behavior, leaving me to drift away once again.

This time I thought about the stinky Chernozem, black fertile soil, and wondered if it still covered the hills behind the building in Odessa where we had lived.

You see, my family had been very lucky: After eight years on a waiting list, while living in a cooperative dwelling with a communal kitchen and a bathroom shared by all tenants, we were finally allowed to move into a two-bedroom apartment of a new building in Cheromushki.

Funny the way things worked back then in Russia. Cheromushki was a new neighborhood in Odessa that consisted of identical gray buildings. After years of bribes to the Communist Party machine, my father, mother, sister and I were finally granted a lottery ticket to win a chance for a new apartment. That was the only way to get stuff in Russia, and not much has changed since then.

What a slap to Lenin's face, who had wanted to get rid of the Tsarist bureaucracy of the Romanovs,

Bribe to Ap (handwritten)

Tsar Nicholas II, and his absolute monarchy over aristocracy, the Church, the police and the Russian army. When Lenin lynched the Romanovs to free the Russian people from being controlled by one monarch, he simply traded him for other Shmoks: Stalin, Khrushchev, Brezhnev....

Yep. My father Emil had to bribe a long line of bureaucrats to get a small two-bedroom apartment. From low-rank clerks all the way up to greedy engineers, my father mastered an innovative way of pleasing a long chain of bureaucrats by providing them with his famous Siberian Sobel mink hats.

You heard me well: My father taught himself how to sew fur hats from the Sobel mink of Siberia. As a result of his creative hard work, after many years residing in one tiny communal room with my great-grandmother Dora, my mother, father, sister and I were granted a two-bedroom walk-up apartment with a small balcony.

In one photo my sister and I, ages ten and eight, stand on the balcony dressed in identical red Kashmir suits decorated with golden beads. My father always managed to bring us fine clothing from his frequent business trips to Moscow and Leningrad (St. Petersburg).

Our building in Cheromushki was situated on a green hill splattered with strokes of wild flowers and random scarlet poppies, white forest violets and the blue bells of forget-me-not flowers.

And after we moved in, there was no happier

family in all Odessa but us, the Skulskis. My father painted the kitchen with murals of French décor he had managed to get from a fashion magazine in Moscow, turning the space airy and light, in spite of only one narrow window looking over the green hills.

My parent's bedroom was smaller than the one my sister and I shared, yet nicely decorated with furniture carved in birch, cherry and oak, their silhouettes mirrored on the hardwood floors my mother waxed daily.

LETTER FOUR: STOLYARSKY

"Are you planning to visit Stolyarsky?" I asked my sister to indicate I was actually paying attention to her non-stop monologue. Without waiting for her answer, I drifted back to the place where I had played my violin until our family left Russia for Israel.

The Stolyarsky School of Music was a Neoclassical building decorated with crystal chandeliers, waxed parquet floors, banisters and moldings. Its walls were covered, floor to ceiling, with portraits of graduated students recognized worldwide, some of whom I was lucky enough to meet.

At Stolyarsky I met famous violinists and conductors such as David Oistrakh and Gidon Kremer, and worked closely with my own teacher, Professor Mordkovitch, a husky man in his late thirties with fair skin, a square freckled face and a mane of red hair. The Stolyarsky School of Music is still a place

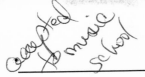

for children with perfect pitch and innate musical gifts; in my case, my musical gift seemed to become my curse as well, because I could never replace and satisfy the lost dreams of others.

After many rigorous exams I was accepted as a Jewish girl into this famous musical academy of Odessa only after many bribes, I'm sure. Professor Mordkovitch was kind and an easily intimidated man. But who could blame him? A Jewish teacher under a Communist regime, he could lose his job by simply befriending anyone who was actively pro West; and my family was tagged as such simply because we wished to move to Israel. Last we met, Professor Mordkovitch wished me good luck in Israel and presented me with a notebook of my favorite melodies.

One time at the Stolyarsky School, my mother and I were approached by a very tall and skinny young man with shiny black hair and thick glasses resting on the tip of his nose. I was sobbing after a very poor performance during my class with Professor Mordkovitch because, of course, I had received a very bad grade.

While staring out the window of my classroom on the second floor of the school, I was startled by this man who tried to comfort me, asking my name and what was wrong. My mother explained that I had just received a very low grade for my performance and was therefore devastated, thus all the quiet sobbing. Smiling warmly, he introduced himself as Gidon Kremer and stated that, even though he was then a relatively famous violinist traveling all over to perform in concerts, nonetheless, when he was about my age of nine years old, he had sometimes done very poorly as well, getting himself into trouble. He advised me never to give up and to keep playing my violin. His advice echoed in my head for many years to come, encouraging and empowering me.

LETTER FIVE: HANNA

So many things blink in front of my eyes that I wish to tell you about, but it is getting harder to remember where to begin. Like the thing about my name. I told you once that everyone back in Odessa called me Anushka, but I did not tell you about my other secret names, one of which was Hanna.

That name was given to me by my paternal grandmother, Polya. Hannah was her mother's name. You see, back in Communist Russia, every new mother was given a notebook with approved names for her newborn baby: Kolya, Vanya, Sasha, Luba, Anna..., but my Grandma Polya's mother's name—Hannah—was not on that list. My family had to choose a similar name from that booklet, and they picked "Anna" from the pretty flower Anutini Glazki, or pansy as you say in English.

So Anna was my name, except to my paternal family, who insisted on calling me Hanna. Then another name came along: I was a very ill baby for the first months of my life. At that point, as per Jewish tradition, my paternal family gave me a second name for my soul: Tabale, a derivative of Tovi, which means "God is good." From that day on, my paternal family called me by my secret Hebrew name Hannah-Tabale, while the rest of the world, including my maternal family—Grandpa Izya and Grandma Valya—called me by my Russian name, Anushka. Someone even mentioned once that Anushka in Sanskrit means grace, lightening and fulfillment of desire. Hm…I am not so sure about that.

Anyhow, that is how it went. Each time I visited my paternal and maternal families I had to adjust and maneuver between the different names each family called me, and it seemed very funny, as though I were acting in a short movie called My Life.

LETTER SIX: GAGA

Having an older sister who was absolutely perfect added even more confusion to my life and did not help me much. My sister was the firstborn, adored by all. She was named Margalit after my paternal grandpa's (Zeida's) mother. Everyone called her Magusha, but she called herself Gaga.

Magusha was born a year and a half before me and was a bundle of endless joy. My maternal grandma, Valya, and Grandpa Izya could not get enough of her perfectly round little face with its cute button-like nose and tiny mouth. One photo shows her with her round face, all smiling, looking much prettier than a huge porcelain doll seated nearby. And from a beautiful baby, my sister grew into a gorgeous, easy-going little toddler who sleepily sat in her carriage or gracefully nibbled on any food at any given time of day.

My sister simply was a doll adored by all. Relatives and friends would Prichmokivali, or purse their lips with pleasure as they watched her cute round face and pinched her rosy cheeks. After a year and a half, to my parent's surprise, I was born. They had obviously no intention of raising a second baby so soon! Not only that, but, unlike my cute older sister, I was nothing but trouble from the very beginning. From a colicky baby who refused food and was unable to thrive, I turned into a toddler who was not at all interested in food and sitting down to eat, but spent hours exploring kitchen cabinets in the home of my poor grandma Valya, managing to maneuver my skinny body into impossible labyrinths stocked with piles of pots, frying pans and plates. My mother said I never walked but flew around like a little bird, carried on my bonny flat feet.

After a while Grandma Valya refused to watch me, declaring she could not keep up with me as I was way too difficult, unlike my sister. My working parents had no choice but to decide that my sister would be watched by Grandma Valya, and I would be sent to my paternal family, to Zeida, Polya, Masha, Miya and Devik, to be looked after.

That decision led to the best time of my childhood; it still echoes as such in my mind, filled with love and amazing adventures.

LETTER SEVEN: VALYA AND IZYA

But first let me tell you about my maternal household in Krasnuy Pereulok, in the Red Corner of Odessa.

The home of my mother's parents—Grandma Valya and Grandpa Izya—was always filled with the fragrance of mouth-watering deep-fried Ponchiks—dumplings filled with meat, potatoes and onion, some with green peas, others filled with sauerkraut or with apples and sweet cherry or another homemade fruit spread and served with chilled sour cream. All that was always available in abundance, ready to feed flocks of family members and guests.

Grandma Valya had many Poslovizi I Pogovorki, or clever sayings and proverbs. Like the one she had when asked How are you? "Ha, Kak V Polshe." "Like in Poland," she would shoot back in a witty reply, referring to the harsh times of impoverished Odessa by jokingly comparing it to neighboring Poland.

Seems oppressed people always find creative ways to express themselves. After all, people in Odessa back then knew very well that merely a joke could send them to the Siberian Gulags, where they could vanish at the hands of the KGB.

My Grandma Valya was known to all for having an arsenal of bull's-eye proverbs, especially during her relentless frying, baking and cooking. How did she manage to raise four children—my mom, Alla; her two sisters, Mery and Bebah; and their youngest brother, Danya (David)—while working full-time at the local supermarket, taking care of her elderly mother, Manya (Malka Schneider) and way too many other relatives to mention here, all of whom resided in that two-room house with its small kitchen and a basement where my grandpa Izya stored his wooden barrels filled with pickles and sauerkraut? That still remains a great mystery to me.

The entire Berdichevski clan resided in their little house located in a neighborhood called Krasnuy Pereulok, Red Block, house number 28, apartment number 3, for over seventy years. Here Valya and Izya raised four children and many grandchildren, and helped other relatives. Their home was very well known in the Odessa community as a hospitable hut in which any newly arrived Jewish family were welcome. Grandma Valya would feed them while Grandpa Izya helped them obtain passports and employment.

The little house in Krasnuy Pereulok had two long rooms connected by a hall with a window and a Raskladushka, or folded bed. The hall was occupied by Great-grandmother Malka Schneider. Manya was assigned this warmest spot of the house since she was in her late eighties. At the end of the hallway, you walked into a small kitchen with a window and walls that were stained with soot from the stove and Valya's constant cooking. Under the window there was a green table always loaded with Kazans, round cast iron pots darkened from years of frying. There were many Kazans in different sizes, filled to the rim with the different Ponchiks, ready for my cousins to come galloping into the house. They would reach out and scoop their hands in to get handfuls of the delicious dumplings, knowing Grandma Valya would keep providing an endless supply.

The house of my grandparents Valya and Izya was always a place to warm up by the iron stove with hot Ponchiks and a cup of sweet tea.

LETTER EIGHT: MEN OF INDUSTRY

While Grandma Valya relentlessly worked in the supermarket and in her kitchen to satisfy the needs of her large family, Grandpa Izya partnered with my father Emil to establish a fashion Atelier, or workshop, on the outskirts of Odessa. To satisfy the demands of youngsters for Western fashion, they produced shiny plastic belts. In one photo, my mother wears one of their red belts at a party. Seems my mom was an amazing PR person: Each time she walked into a room wearing the red belt with her small black dress, her hair in a platinum-blond Brigitte Bardot style of the '60s, Grandpa and my father were bombarded by tons of orders for the same red belt.

Besides plastic belts for silly teenagers, the Atelier also satisfied greedy demands of fat clerks and old-fart generals for the Sobel mink hats my father had taught himself to sew from the fur he obtained from Siberia. My mom was always frightened he might not return back home from those trips, but he always managed to charm the soldiers with bottles of vodka and a few rubles. Only once I remember he came back with gauze on his ear. "Ha…, just like Van Gogh," my father said, joking around for losing part of his earlobe to freezing Siberia. A small price to pay for Sobel mink fur, he said.

Can you imagine the courage and charisma Grandpa Izya and my father Emil had to have to run a business in the '60s behind the Iron Curtain of Communist Odessa?! It's a miracle they both managed to avoid vanishing into the Gulags of the Siberian tundra.

As a result of this insane entrepreneurship, our families enjoyed a high-end lifestyle and went away for entire summers in order to fly low under the Party's radar. We cruised each summer in the Caucasus Mountains with its many lakes and palaces, and sometimes we flew to Moscow. In one photo from one of our trips to Moscow, an elegant man in his early thirties, my father, wears a wool suit with a silk tie and a platinum pin with matching cufflinks. He stands by my mother, who is dressed in a black gown accessorized with a crocodile-leather belt and matching shoes.

My father always managed to find the most exotic places for us to visit. Another photo shows my mother and sister eating local fish in a mid-air restaurant that hangs above the blue waters of a beautiful lake. The table is surrounded by peacocks which I chase, under my mother's disapproving gaze. Who could eat fried fish, no matter how exotic, while the peacocks marched around, spreading their brilliant feathers of all colors?!

LETTER NINE: Reprieves

Spending the summers with family was a great reprieve for my parents: My father could generously tip everyone as Mom finally enjoyed her locked-away diamonds she could never wear back in Odessa. She could also dress my sister and me in the fine silk clothing we were allowed to wear only behind closed doors at home. Why, you ask? Because one day a neighbor asked my mother where our silk was coming from, and how my engineer father could afford to buy such outfits. (Engineers, doctors and shoemakers all had equal incomes under Communist rule back then. All for one and one for all. Stupid &^% bastards.)

After the neighbor made such comments, my mother made sure to dressed us in gray skirts identical to those worn by other local girls. And when my sister and I were visiting our school friends and offered macaroni and plain cheese, we had to pretend to be excited to eat a hot meal. We were never allowed to invite friends over to share our daily meals of caviar, meat and fresh eggs out of fear our neighbors would rat us out.

It must be hard for Americans to understand all that, since they are born in this amazing land of freedom, but Russia was a very dark place ruled by an iron fist of dictators and the secret agency of the KGB, all of whom wished to suffocate any notions of free thinking. They were also the only ones to enjoy wearing mink Sobel hats during frozen winter, and to be driven around by private chauffeurs in black Moskvitch cars.

Emil, Maga, Alla and Anushka
Crimea-Batumi 1969

LETTER TEN: MEIR DAVIDOVICH SKULSKI—ZEIDA

As day and night complement each other, so did my paternal household of Zeida, Polya, and Miya complement my maternal household of Valya and Izya. Located in the Ostrovidova 97 Street, on the second floor, it stood across from the #100 building where David Oistrakh grew up studying to play violin with the same teacher who instructed my father. Famed violinist Olga Borisovna was renowned for identifying child prodigies. Part of David Oistrakh's training involved preparing for the rigorous entrance exam at the Stolyarsky School of Music, the same school I would one day enter.

My father had me tested with Olga when I turned five. I remember a lady with short gray hair and a round face. After testing my hearing, singing and the structure of my hands, she identified me as a child prodigy with inner musical talents to develop. It seems my tiny hands were very flexible and the gaps between my fingers provided for a wide spread that would allow me to reach the highest notes.

Just as David Oistrakh was tested at age five was I tested too, as was my father Emil before me. More circles.

My paternal grandparents' apartment was on the third floor of an old building situated in a quiet tree-lined neighborhood near the City Park. Upon my arrival, my Aunt Miya and Grandma Polya always greeted me on the staircase with wild open arms and impish smiles that held the promise of adventure. Behind a solid wood door, a narrow hallway with dark oak parquet floors led to a small bedroom on the right that was occupied by Aunt Miya and her son, Devik. A glass door at the end of the hall opened into a living room with a high ceiling, moldings and two huge windows that brought in plenty of daylight. The room also served as a dining area as well as a study, and had wrap-around walls of glass-door walnut cabinets full of piles of books. Faint echoes of music bounced from an old radio into the walls, which always seemed to whisper the secrets of the house.

LETTER ELEVEN: ZEIDA'S STUDENTS

Drifting back in time to Zeida's living room, I can see there about a dozen young and enthusiastic men seated by the oval table. They have arrived one by one in order to avoid raising neighbors' suspicions. Those were Zeida's students. After a long day at the university they always managed to stop by, hungry and cold, to spend a few hours with Zeida to learn Hebrew and share in mutual concerns for Odessa's Jews. Heavy curtains snuggled around double-glass windows insulated the apartment from the freezing Russian winter, shielding us from spying neighbors who might rat us out to the secret militia of the KGB.

It must be very difficult to understand nowadays, but back then in Russia even listening to the West was considered a betrayal to the People, the Communist Party.

Yet, against all odds back in Communist Odessa, my grandfather Meir Davidovich Skulski, called by all "Zeida," established the first secret Ulpan (school for the intensive study of Hebrew) in Odessa in

1964, and ran it until 1971 (Zal'') in his apartment at Ostrovidova 97 Street.

LETTER TWELVE: ULPAN

Each time I visited my paternal home, Grandfather Zeida was involved in a major adventure, novelty of surprise, or mystery with risks. He opened for us all a world of secrets and discoveries wrapped with heavy curtains of mystery, away from the outside world.

Once I walked into that apartment, the darkness was left outside and all that remained was pure wonder: chants of soft-spoken people and fragrances of Aunt Miya's pan-fried potatoes. Zeida's living room was transformed into a safe haven from 1964 until May 1971. It was an Eden as the first Ulpan in Communist Odessa, a secret school where young Jewish students arrived for weekly lessons orchestrated by Zeida so they could study the Hebrew language as well as the literature and music of their people, all forbidden by Communist authorities who would deprive them of such knowledge.

For seven years, once a week, a group of young people arrived to fill their hungry minds with Hebrew literature and the heritage and the future of the Jewish people in Russia. Many years of debates left Zeida with only one logical resolution: the inevitable return of a young Jewish generation to the one place they could call Home. And these weekly meetings ultimately transformed his young students into people with renewed hope to reach the place where they truly belonged: Israel.

Behind the curtains of the crowded living room, the eager Jewish students gathered around Zeida, all attentively staring at a box and listening to…absolute silence. Nothing. And after the longest silence, none of us daring to speak or eat the now-cold pan-fried potatoes, suddenly to our relief a scratchy noise came from the box. It was a brown lacquered box, its front wrapped in yellow tapestry with three wooden knobs in the middle.

After a while the cacophony turned into soft murmurs and, eventually, into fascinating translations by Zeida, each of which evoked excitement and debates to be shushed by the next squeaks from the box, which were then followed by silence until Zeida spoke again.

With each new strange sound from the box, my heart jumped out of excitement for another mystery. Eventually someone whispered "BBC…." What an adventure…! It was almost as good as the red-hair cat we called Stalin and those fried potatoes Aunt Miya made for us on the iron stove. How did Zeida manage to capture the broadcast from the WEST, from London, with so many ever-spying neighbors? This remains yet another mystery of my childhood.

On several occasions during which I slept overnight there, I heard strange noises and was told it was nothing but the cat. But Zeida was gone the next morning and the apartment seemed cold and foreign for days until he returned, looking awful, dragging his feet yet alive.

What did they want? Who knows what the KGB was searching for at Zeida's apartment at such times? Did they expect to find a traitor, a spy? Or maybe the red-hair cat was to blame for such visits; Miya said I should never call him outside the apartment by his name, Stalin.

Word of the Ulpan spread quickly and, after a while, more and more people began arriving at Zeida's apartment; some out of curiosity, others as spies, but a few of them turned into a loyal group who would meet for years to come. They were introduced to Zeida by his friend Boris Gimelfarb, who met a few of the young men at a concert of Nehama Lifshitz, a National Jewish freedom advocate (who currently resides in Israel, eighty-five years young and a lovely lady).

The group was comprised of young men, most with wives: Lyona and Ina, Petya and Mara, Izya and Zenya, my father Emil (Zeida's son) and Alla, plus Nahum, who was not married at the time. Many of these people would eventually reside in Israel!

In this group of dedicated students one stood alone: Naum Slopack, a young man in his thirties and a talented photographer. His friends called him Nahum. An avid activist of freedom, he did whatever he could to spread around Jewish culture as he copied forbidden poetry, studied books and records from Israel and turned out to be one of the most prominent of Zeida's students. Nahum was the first to master the Hebrew language, as well as the first of us to be allowed to go to Israel by the KGB. He was considered our hero.

It was great to see my Zeida basking in the warmth of the surrounding young men, who also enjoyed the warm hospitality and fragrant pan-fried potatoes Grandma Polya and Aunt Miya prepared. While my grandmother and aunt fed the hungry students' stomachs, Zeida fed their hungry souls.

Floor-to-ceiling cabinets were stocked with books by Voltaire, Spinoza, Plato, Shimon Frug, Ilf and Petrov, Boris Pasternak, Rabindranath Tagore…. Zeida and Grandma Polya were avid readers; both were also fluent in Hebrew, Yiddish, German, Rashi, and Aramaic languages. I think Zeida may have also known a few other languages, Arabic perhaps, but I am not sure.

Once when I came across an old book Zeida said, "Read Voltaire, Anushka," and gave me a playful smirk. I never knew when he was serious or just kidding; I guess he never took himself too seriously.

For more than twenty-five years Zeida was on the faculty at the Financial Institute of Odessa, where he lectured about accounting and economics. He was also an avid activist with the Zionist Organization of Odessa. In November 1903 Zeida was sent as a delegate representing the organization to the Kharkov Conference, a protest conference of Russian Zionists. It would be followed by the Sixth

Zionist Congress at which Theodor Herzl proposed
Uganda as a place of asylum for the Jews.

Meir Davidovich Skulski, Zeida
Odessa 1937

LETTER THIRTEEN: STISHOK

But what do I really know about my Zeida, my
cool grandfather? Drifting away once again, slipping through the cracks of time, I look at another
photo: I am about five years old, skinny, with short
wavy brown hair, curious eyes, a pointy nose covered
with freckles, a few missing front teeth. Zeida gently
holds me on a chair in the living room, surrounded
by familiar smiling faces: Lyona, Petya, Izya, Naum,

my mother Alla and my father Emil. Aunt Miya is sitting on the soft divan, which is upholstered with fading yet still-soft and colorful taffeta silk. In a storage box underneath the divan she always kept my cousin Devik's brown corduroy bear with one glass eye.

I am standing on the chair while everyone waits to hear a few lines of a Stishok, a children's poem, I have memorized for my Zeida: "HameShanimAvruLeMichaelBeLimudim...." "Five years Michael spent by studying...," I proclaimed out loud, filled with pride, breathlessly connecting all the strange sounds into one long and fuzzy line that resembled a caterpillar I once found at the park with Aunt Miya.

LETTER FOURTEEN: ZEIDA

There are so many stories to tell about my Zeida, a beloved teacher and community leader. An academically trained professor of economics, he spent his long career at the Odessa Financial Institute. Then, after twenty-eight years when it was time for him to retire, Zeida did something remarkable. A common Communist Party procedure was to have a retiree sign a paper thanking Stalin and the Communist Party for all his life achievements as an acknowledgement of the Party's role as the main and only source of a successful career. Mind you, back in those oppressed days, Zeida—a Jewish professor— was under constant scrutiny and experienced much humiliation from KGB agents. And now they were asking him to thank them by signing the biggest lie of his life?! Bastards.

You know what happens next, don't you? Zeida refused to sign the paper, and the KGB denied him his modest retirement pension of a few rubles every month for the rest of his life, letting his family barely survive in already impoverished Russia. That is the kind of man my Zeida was: a true patriarch who would not do anything that contradicted his values.

Everyone called him Zeida, not just me; even his own family. Growing up, I thought it was his name until my Aunt Miya (my father's sister) told me his real name was Meir Davidovich (son of David) Skulski. Later on, Zeida added another name to his own, Paulinov, out of love to his wife, my grandmother Polya (Pearl-Lea), who was his complementing pearl, just as his beloved Odessa was the pearl by the Black Sea. Grandma Polya was indeed an equal partner in all merits, fluent in so many languages…. Their union was comprised of great love, friendship and mutual respect.

LETTER FIFTEEN: BABUSHKA POLYA

My father's mother, Pearl-Lea, was known to all as Polya. Babushka (Grandmother) Polya always captured my imagination with many vivid stories that fascinated me as a child. Later on, she taught me how to dance the waltz; Strauss was our favorite. Her favorite flower was red carnations and her favorite color was a deep moss green. It is the color of a skirt she wears in a photo I have of her and her sister, Masha.

When Aunt Miya and Grandmother Polya finally came to Israel, they were granted a two-bedroom apartment on the second floor of a building near the beach. They lived merely a few minutes away from the pink long building where my family lived. Their kitchen window faced the sea and their living room had a narrow balcony frequently visited by pigeons and seagulls that feasted on breadcrumbs Babushka Polya left for them. Surely this reminded her of her beloved Odessa, by the Black Sea, where she fed pigeons in the local park she strolled daily with Zeida, holding his elbow in the old-fashioned way. Her plain metal bed she got from the absorption office of Sohnut in Israel was covered with a moss-green silk cloth decorated with delicate flowers of jasmine and mimosa. She knew how much I adored this spread and promised to leave it for me as a gift when she died, but I never had the courage to ask for it from Aunt Miya. She loved it, too.

I loved to spend my time in that apartment, listening to my grandmother Polya, looking at her wrinkled face, trying to see in her wrinkles all that had happened in her life. And her stories were truly fascinating, like the one about the Pogroms or massacres of the Jews by Cossacks in 1903, when she saw her village burned down to ashes, limbs from severed bodies everywhere. She had nightmares about it until her death at the age of eighty-five: the same Cossacks, the same bloody visions of her burning village and so many smashed, bleeding bodies.

She also loved to talk about the last Russian emperor, Tsar Nikolai the II, "Nicki" as she fondly called him. I always wondered if he ever really visited Odessa riding in a golden carriage, yet at the same time I enjoyed this story and did not really mind much that it might not have really happened. I tell you, Babushka Polya was a great storyteller, just like the Brothers Grimm.

There were many stories, some of which were sad and others which simply took my breath away. Like the one about Babushka Polya getting accepted as the only Jewish girl in Odessa, during the time of Tsar Nicki, into a prestigious academy for young ladies. The school was the only one of its kind in Odessa, and there she became fluent in many languages: German, English, French, and later Yiddish and Hebrew. But she never told me about graduating with honors and receiving a solid gold medal. Aunt Miya was the one who told me about it, adding that the gold was taken away during the war. I call it STOLEN by the Nazis, or the Romanians, or the ugly cleaning maintenance people, who also cleaned all the apartments of any valuable items. But we never talked about it, as we never talked about many other things.

Aunt Miya later told me that the same maintenance man who took the gold medal also took Miya's own white baby grand piano, Polya's fur and the little savings they had. All that disappeared from their apartment upon the family's return from Uzbekistan, where they were evacuated during the war. After the war, when Zeïda, Miya, Polya, and little Emil (my father) returned to Odessa to their apartment on the second floor of Ostrovidova 97, everything was gone; the apartment was empty. But one day Grandmother Polya saw Dvornik, a man who swept the building's yard, carrying HER fur for HIS ugly fat wife. My grandma did not say a word. She was a real lady. And later on, Aunt Miya told me a secret: Once she saw her white baby grand piano at the same maintenance man's apartment on the first floor, below their apartment; she had glanced inside as the door opened wide when she was passing by. Miya asked me never to mention a word to Grandma Polya, her mom. Of course I kept my word, not quite understanding and angry at the maintenance man who had stolen my aunt's piano.

LETTER SIXTEEN: TIME IS TICKING

After Zeïda retired and the Party deprived him of his pension, he could no longer keep bottled up all his profound frustration and concerns for the society in which he lived. But his greatest concern was for his fellow Jewish people who were suffering under such an oppressive regime. He decided to look for people of a similar mindset, people with whom he could share his concerns for the future of the Jewish people living in Communist Russia.

After some time, Zeïda managed to surround himself with a loyal group of friends: Boris Gimelfarb, the poet Yohanan Giterman, his students Naum Slopack and Lyona Shaltz. He shared with these friends his vision, frequently read poems and discussed Kabala, Socrates, Voltaire.... One of his favorite paragraphs was from the Mishnah by Hillel the Elder: "...in ein ani li mi li...ve im lo akhshav ematai...leazmi az me ani...."

Zeida also read many poems by Shimon Frug (1860–1916), the national Jewish poet, lyricist and author. Zeida told us once how, shaken by the pogroms of 1881-82, Frug joined the Hibat Zion (Love of Zion) movement. His poem "Jewish Melody" turned into an anthem and he became regarded as the national Jewish poet of Russia. When Frug died in Odessa, more than 100,000 people attended his funeral march! That is how my Zeida was: always talking about the greatness of others. He never mentioned the fact that he knew so many languages, most of them self-taught.

When Zeida was seventy, a few years short of dying from cancer, I remember him wearing his corduroy brown jacket with stiches on the elbows and sitting by the oak dining room table, surrounded by shelves of books. He was tapping his foot and chanting strange words as he passed his index finger over funny symbols on a piece paper. "Japanese," he said, following my wide eyes. When I asked "Why Japanese?" Zeida looked back at me with his own piercing eyes and said, "Time is ticking, so I may as well." I could not understand how time can tick: Did it hide inside the wall clock, or was it hiding inside

Zeida's pocket watch? It was impossible to know when Zeida was joking or was dead serious.

Surely by now it is easy for you to see how growing up with the Skulski clan gave me the most fascinating, rich and loving environment possible. There was no place like their apartment and I could never get enough of them. No fancy car, Baroque pearls or bullions of gold could ever replace the kind of rich environment Zeida shared as he offered his pearls of wisdom. The freezing apartment at Ostrovidova 97 Street was always filled with eager minds ready to inhale the collective wisdom of the People of six thousand years ago, and Zeida was always happy to share it.

LETTER SEVENTEEN: ACACIA TREES

Strolling city parks with my father's sister, Aunt Miya, was always a new adventure because she knew each name of every tree and shrub, as well as a story or two to tell. Humble and a bit shy, Aunt Miya would sometimes play me a concerto or sonata on her black fortepiano in the living room of Ostrovidova Street 97.

Years later I learned she graduated with honors in biology from Mechnikov Odessa National University and worked as an adjunct professor there! Miya remains an enigma, as my entire paternal family does. She spoke few words and held close never-to-be-mentioned names with many secrets.

During one of our walks, Aunt Miya pointed to

a plant, stating it was an acacia tree that is also called
a koa tree in the Hawaiian language, which translates
into a "brave and fearless warrior."

"Acacia is part of the mimosa family of plants,"
Aunt Miya said, pointing out the similarity in char-
acteristics of both plants with fuzzy flowers. Meanwhile I was trying not to giggle too much at a tickling
fuzzy caterpillar I carried in my palm. Later, while
visiting the Hawaiian Islands, I would see the koa
trees that resemble much of the acacia from Odessa.
Miya always had a mesmerizing story to tell, and this
one was no different.

"Anochka," she continued, filling my heart with
great expectations for another adventure, "only a
few people know that the acacia tree is also called
the Hashitta Tree in Hebrew. It is the same tree that
supplied the Shittim-wood in Exodus that was used
to build the Tabernacle, and…"—Miya pointed her
index finger to indicate even greater secrecy—"…
the same Shitta-tree wood from the Torah told in
the story of Moses and the burning bush!" Wow,
that was even a better adventure than ever, I said
to myself. How can it be that the common fragrant
acacia growing all over Odessa was actually from
the ancient times of Moses?! How I wished to share
this discovery with my friends from the Stolyarsky
School of Music, but Miya said it was our new secret, and it was even more dangerous than the secret
about Devik's red-hair cat.

Once I called the cat's name from the porch of
the apartment at Ostrovidova 97. I was just calling

the cat by his name—Stalin—so he could come eat.
I knew how much my cousin Devik loved him and
would want him fed. Little did I know such an act
would cause a look of horror to appear on Miya's
face and stares from so many neighbors! Such mis-
takes were not to be made in Communist Odessa in
the 1970s.

LETTER EIGHTEEN: AUNT MIYA

I spent many magical afternoons with Aunt
Miya, listening to her stories filled with jokes and
laughs. One of my favorite pastimes was to stroll
with her in the local park, down the block from the
apartment on Ostrovidova 97. We would collect wild
chestnuts, acorns and leaves during October, when
the air was crisp and fresh, the park filled with aged
trees, the ground covered with rustling leaves, the
faint fragrance of the fall stirring all around as the
trees stood tall and still, their branches heavy with
pine cones, wild chestnuts and acorns.

Upon returning to the apartment we would read
a story or two, then make out of clay little gnomes
who came alive when we connected acorns with the
branches collected at the park, or turn the leaves into
a classified herbarium by pressing them between
newspaper under a heavy book. There was no TV or
internet like you have nowadays, when so many kids
have their own computers and flat-screen TVs in
their bedrooms for privacy. How silly; privacy from
what?

Zeida's apartment had only two bedrooms: Miya and Devik lived in one, and the other bedroom by the kitchen and the bathroom was occupied by Zeida and Polya. Devik's bicycle was always hanging on the hall wall behind the main door. And his fat cat, red-hair Stalin, was always trying to sneak out.

Inside the apartment a small radio played soft music as we did our early morning session of exercises. Zeida promoted healthy lifestyles and physical activity. In the middle of the living room was an oval wooden table covered with a white plastic cloth. Miya always kept a few candies wrapped in shiny metal paper of red, green, yellow and silver colors. After eating the candy, I would place the crumpled wrap on the tablecloth and very carefully smooth it out with my fingernail, as Miya once showed me. You see how clever she was?

I had many of those smooth small squares of colorful metallic paper under the plastic tablecloth. Later on, during long winter afternoons, we would make window decorations from all that paper by cutting different shapes of snowflakes and gluing them onto an old newspaper. We did not go to Kmart or Walmart to buy supplies as you do now.

Miya was very resourceful and could make everything from nothing. Once she showed me how to make my own crown just like the one worn by Snegurochka, a snow maiden from Russian fairy tales. And this is how I learned to make a crown using white paper, glue, a fluff of cotton and sparkly colorful metallic papers from my collection under the tablecloth. How pretty it was. Sometimes, if I had many squares under the tablecloth, I would take an entire whole square, crumple it into a ball and glue it in the middle of the crown like a jewel.

Once the crowns were done, Aunt Miya and I placed them inside the doubled-glass windows, trying in vain to keep the warm air radiating from the apartment's iron stove from slipping out. Aunt Miya would then make a fake angry face, grab a bucket and shovel and, laughing, we would both go down to the building basement to dig up a pile of coal.

Back in the apartment, we could never resist drawing silly faces with our ashy hands, under the disapproving stare of Grandma Polya. Then I would be told to place a chunk of black coal inside Pechka, the iron stove, which was in the middle of the living room, and Miya would bake a potato or two for dinner. And those were the best potatoes I ever ate, with burned skin, fresh butter and sprinkled coarse salt! Hmm…. These were just some of many adventures with my Aunt Miya.

Like the one when she took an old black nail and turned it into a bright scarlet color in front of my eyes, simply by dipping it into a glass filled with stinky water. Of course she was teaching me chemistry, but I was about six or so and simply fascinated by my pretty Aunt Miya and her magic.

Like I said, Aunt Miya knew a great deal about making stuff from nothing. She could make only one pair of socks last forever with a few magic needle strokes. She would stretch the sock on a wooden stick with a mushroom head and then stitch over the hole. I would watch as she made small strokes and, as by magic, make the hole disappear.

"Do you want to try?" she said one day. And that is how I learned to stitch when I was six.

While strolling through Odessa, Aunt Miya and I often visited my favorite place, the Prince Vorontsov Palace, "built by Sardinian architect Francesco Boffo in the nineteenth century." Miya used to copy tour leaders, finalizing our tour with a treat of Plombir V Shokolade, chocolate ice cream, once we reached the street of Deribasovskaya. Similar to our Fifth Avenue in Manhattan, Deribasovskaya was "built by the De Rivas brothers in the heart of Odessa," Miya kept enlightening me while I consumed the ice cream. But I was thinking only about the funny word "Sardinian" that sounds the same as a fish.

In one of my photos a pretty smiling lady in her early thirties sits gracefully, queen like, next to a little boy with dark curls; the photo is of Aunt Miya with my little cousin Devik. See how gorgeous Aunt Miya was with her black thick hair, smooth tan skin, warm dark eyes and pencil-painted lips? Many people would turn around to stare at her as we strolled through the Gorodskoy Park, the City Park in Odessa, after she picked me up from the Stolyarsky School. And at the Opera, where she often took me, people paid more attention to my pretty aunt than to the performers on the stage. She was the center of attention, just like a movie star. There was no end to my joy and pride as I walked by her side, basking in her warmth, elegance and beauty, listening to her chatty speech. But there were a few names Aunt Miya seldom chatted about.

Miya and Devik
Odessa 1964

LETTER NINETEEN: KARLUSHA

One photo shows Zeida, Polya, Karlusha and little Miya; my father Emil was not born yet. They are all smiling, nicely dressed in traditional clothing, Zeida and Karlusha with caps and Polya with a small piece of lace covering her brown wavy hair.

Another photo shows a young soldier wearing a dusty uniform and a blank stare: Karlusha. I always wondered what made my Uncle Karl Skulski, Karlusha, pause medical school to go fight the German Nazis. But each time Karlusha's name was mentioned, Grandma Polya would leave the room with red eyes and shaky hands. Karlusha had turned into a ghost no one dared to bring up. But that did not prevent me from puzzling about all that had happened.

How was it possible for my Uncle Karlusha to become a fighter pilot at the age of eighteen after only a few weeks of training? After all, he wanted to become a doctor like his Aunt Masha, his mother's sister. Were the Red Army people blinded by patriotism, naively believing that a young medical student could master the skills of a fighter pilot in a week or two, that they could instantly transform Karlusha into a skillful Russian Kamikaze? Was it just a stagnant Communist regime luring the young and brightest into unrealistic training? Or perhaps it was plain incompetency on behalf of the Party, which sent freshly trained pilots to fight a German fleet armed with the best technology and the most skillful pilots.

Luckily I am not in the Odessa of my Grandma Polya; I would vanish in Siberia for even thinking all that, but that is the truth of what happened to Karlusha. During the first week of the war, following a short training period, Karlusha crashed his plane on the Caucasus Mountain ridge, which overlooks the picturesque city of Nalchik that was then occupied by Germans as a strategic point on the Crimean Peninsula. And every summer when my family went on an Ivan Franco cruise around Crimea and the Caucasus Mountains, my father (who was three years old when Karlusha was killed) would look for the place that might still hold the remains of his older brother, so he could return with them for a proper funeral back home in Odessa.

One photo shows a bronze monument topped with a red star near an eternal flame burning in the city of Nalchik. Erected in 1947, it commemorated the burial place of 138 soldiers who perished in the fights of Nalchik when it was occupied by the Germans. Karlusha was among them, but his remains were never recovered. And the bronze star of the monument was blown off later by Chechnyan soldiers; I may have the only photo that remains. All my requests to go visit Nalchik have been turned down by the local authorities of that troubled region.

Karlusha was never mentioned in Zeida's apartment, joining other ghosts of the Skulski clan. Like that of the first-born daughter, little Yehudith, who died of meningitis at the age of four, though once someone said she actually died of a horrible accident no one talked about. Her name was never mentioned, either.

There were many ghost in Zeida's apartment, and once I met one of them: Her name was Gusta.

Karl Skulski, medical student
Odessa 1941

LETTER TWENTY: Gusta

Grandma Polya had two younger sisters: Gusta and Maria Somoylovna Tikh, affectionately known by everyone as Masha. But no one ever mentioned the other sister, Gusta.

Her name was omitted during holidays and family gatherings, forbidden ever to be spoken as if she had never even existed. But one day, under great secrecy, Aunt Miya showed me a black and white photo of three young girls: "Polya, Masha and Gusta," she said. Pretty and young, the sisters were well dressed in long lace dresses and wore pearl necklaces.

Miya later told me how Gusta went mad, completely losing her mind as a young bride who lost her newly wed husband during World War II. Shortly after telling me this, Aunt Miya took me with her, out from the apartment under a lame excuse, to meet HER.

My heart violently pounded, threatening to burst, as I watched Aunt Miya purchase a brown bag filled with square tea biscuits for "hungry and cold Gusta," she whispered softly. "It has to be our secret, Anushka," Miya added with a wink of conspiracy, adding Gusta's name to the many others we were forbidden to mention to Polya. From that day on, once in a while Aunt Miya and I would sneak out for a bag of tea biscuits, and to meet with a tall and skinny woman with messy long hair and huge hazel eyes that stared at something only she could see.

Gusta was another painful family ghost, one that even her own sister, Dr. Maria Tikh—my Masha— could not save.

LETTER TWENTY-ONE: MASHA SAVES ANUSHKA

Now I will share with you some of the stories my mom told me about Masha: my grandma Polya's sister.

I was born with many ailments that prevented my body from digesting food, which resulted in a vitamin deficiency and lack of growth. Both my parents worked full-time, and my older sister stayed with Grandma Valya, whose hands were full already with her own full-time job plus caring for a large family. She could not dedicate much time to a sick baby.

During that time, Masha (Dr. Maria Tikh) returned from Berlin and assumed the position of Director of the Center for Disease Control department in the Odessa Hospital. But Masha had a second job, as well: After long days spent saving lives at the hospital, she also dedicated all her attention and love to saving a sick baby—me.

My working parents let Grandma Polya and Miya take care of me during the day. Then, upon returning home from work, Masha (who stayed at Zeida's apartment after the war), took me for a daily stroll for fresh air and a dose of vitamin D from the sun. She also insisted on feeding me only freshly squeezed juice from the Concord grapes she specially got weekly from the Caucasus Mountains of Uzbekistan. She trusted that the fertile soil of the valleys would provide needed nutrients to clean my anemic body, renewing and replacing my blood.

My mom told me that "every fifteen minutes around the clock, Masha would squeeze into your little mouth a few drops of fresh grape juice…and she kept repeating it all over after you threw it all up." Not giving up, Masha insisted on her course of healing and, after a while, to everyone's amazement, my blood got better, my anemia subsided and it seemed that all the juicing had saved my life, after all. Soon my vision and fine motor skills improved and I acquired better eating habits.

All this time my poor mom must have been comparing my skinny body to the healthy body of my older sister, horrified as any young mother would be. My sister had a round face with chubby cheeks and could eat two or three servings of Mannaya Kasha, farina porridge, with chunks of butter. One photo shows my sister and me seated on a couch. It seems I was a pretty OK child, quite regular in size, but when I was compared to my sister, my mother must have been very embarrassed, thinking that maybe people thought she did not feed me as well as she fed my sister.

The first word I said was: "Maha." Masha.

Another photo shows my Masha with her deep hazel eyes, her long brown hair neatly combed in a bun. She always carried a few pieces of my favorite candy, a red ruby-colored hard candy called Barbariska.

Masha did not have children of her own, not because of a lack of opportunities, but because she had to obey the patriarch of the family. Everyone had to obey the family patriarch back then, unlike today when kids always ask why this, why that and argue and talk back. As the oldest living male and therefore the family patriarch, Zeida forbade his sister-in-law's marriage to a non-Jewish gentleman, a handsome doctor (my mom once told me) with whom Masha had fallen in love during the war, and whose only sin was not being a Jew.

By marrying a non-Jew, Masha would have gone

against all that Zeida believed in. He was, after all, preparing his friends and family to go away from oppressed Russia and back Home, to the land of the Jewish People, Israel.

Masha (left) and Polya (right)
Odessa 1913

My Masha died of a heart attack after her doctor married a lovely Russian lady. "A broken heart," my mom said with teary eyes. My mother always felt bad for Masha's destiny as a veteran doctor, returned back home to spend her last years living on Zeida's couch. Mom had had big plans for Masha: Once the government assigned us an apartment, Masha would move in with us. But when we finally got our apartment in Cheromushki, it was too late for Masha. On

November 11, 1964, my Masha was buried after she died of a broken heart. Zeida had only one word to say by her grave: "Prosti." Forgive me.

Dr. Mariya Tikh (Masha) on the
left with fellow doctor
Berlin 1946

LETTER TWENTY-TWO: CRYING SKIES

And now there is no way around sharing sad memories from the day of Zeida's funeral. What choice do I have? If I don't tell you, who will? And once I am gone all will disappear and you will never know about our family.

May 1, 1971 was a rainy day. I sat in a car with Miya and Polya as we followed a long black car with

Zeida's coffin to the old Jewish cemetery of Odessa in nearby Tolkuchka.

Everyone said the skies were crying for all of us, for the loss of our teacher and leader. And all I could think of was Zeida's jokes and how he would probably have laughed at all that, telling me that if the sky was crying, he surely did not need a few more drops from my tears, and I better keep them for days without rain. Little did I know how many dry days were on the horizon, creeping crawling, unpredictable as Life.

When my Zeida passed away (Zal") on May 1, 1971, the Ulpan was over. A month later, my family of four (my parents, my sister and I) became the first family from Zeida's Ulpan to be allowed to leave Russia. Other families would follow, including those of Lyona Shultz, a talented young engineer and Ina Shultz (Zal"), a kind and sweet piano teacher survived by many grandchildren; and Petya Golger (Zal"), a dentist survived by two sons, a daughter and his wife Mara. (People say Mara is currently serving as dean of the London Tech, but I am not sure of that. You know people like to gossip. All I know is that she was a prominent engineer who studied physics.) Zeida would have been very proud to know of his beloved students and their many grandchildren who currently reside at Home, living a life of free people in Israel.

But Zeida did not make it: In May 1971, Zeida was buried in the old Jewish cemetery of Odessa he had frequently visited with friends to talk about the rich Jewish community prior to the war. He was buried there among the many famous poets, scientists and doctors he had loved to discuss.

His friend Boris Gimelfarb wrote about the cemetery in an article published in a Jerusalem newspaper: "Looking at that old photo you can see a few steps from Meir Davidovich Skulski's modest tomb the resting place of the mother of the great poet Shaul Tshernihovskiy, and a little further the resting place of Mendale 'the book peddler,' born Sholem Yankev Abramovich (1835-1917), a Jewish poet and one of the founders of modern Yiddish and Hebrew literature. And a few steps away is the resting place of Professor Bardah, who established the first Russian EMS service.

"And near there you'll find the resting place of the national Jewish poet Shimon Frug, whose modest tombstone was arranged by Zeida himself just one year prior to his own funeral; he had the local mason engrave two words 'Shimon Frug' in Hebrew letters, since the original marble monument was taken away during the Romanian occupation with other Jewish monuments to Bucharest. And here, as you see in this photo of overgrown shrubs and wild bushes, you can hardly see, but look closely: There is an old stone dedicated to the men, women and babies butchered during the pogroms of 1905 and during the German and Romanian occupations.

"Although the tomb is almost concealed by vegetation, it cannot cover the horrors of the Odessa Massacre, where over 100,000 Jews were shot or burned in the area between the Dniester and Bug Rivers (including Babi Yar) in 1941-42."

LETTER TWENTY-THREE: MISSING ZEIDA

After the funeral we all returned to Ostrovidova 97 Street, Zeida's apartment, where we gathered in the living room. And for the first time in my life, to my amazement, I saw my father Emil's cheeks drenched with tears as he leaned on the wall and began to tremble and descend all the way down to the floor. And he was not the only one. Scattered people were choking as though they were fish out of water, fearing the unknown future that hovered over the apartment. The leader was gone and now what? Ghost-like people walked around, rubbing their red eyes and scratching their pale faces. The room was filled with sobbing. People whispered in despair about losing an anchor, and all future hope.

Watching the grown-ups turned into scared children made me realize for the first time what my Zeida meant to others, besides being my Zeida, my funny, smart and amusing grandpa. "He was never my Zeida all alone," I concluded. He belonged to so many others. As much as I disliked that notion of sharing my grandpa, that was my inevitable conclusion. Then a less-flattering thought surfaced. It was difficult to resist thinking about the fact that, while Zeida was giving away himself to others, he often did not have time to address the needs of his immediate family. Why would he selflessly give himself to others…? What about Masha, Emil, Devik, Miya…? Frantic thoughts kept rising in my mind, building into a snowball of anger. And what about me? What about Anushka? What about Pochemuchka, "Why," as my father fondly used to call me.

LETTER TWENTY-FOUR: LET MY PEOPLE GO

Then happened the most extraordinary thing: In June 1971, one month after we buried Zeida, my father was summoned to appear at the headquarters of the KGB. My mother waited by the window all day long, frightened she would never see him again. But there he was, with a broad smile, holding a package of baked goods, fresh flowers and some papers. "Start packing," he said, and Mom did not know whether to cry or to laugh.

My father Emil explained the KGB had summoned him to provide our family with a visa for our IMMEDIATE departure from Odessa. Hmm… sounds like they were kicking us out. Of course, there was a catch: Grandmother Polya, Aunt Miya and cousin Devik were not allowed to join us. There was another catch: Each of us—my mother, sister, father and I—were allowed to carry whatever we wanted inside only TWO suitcases.

Suddenly, just like that! After years of harassing Zeida for his longing to leave for Israel and a whole year of refusing to let us go, all of a sudden the government had made us the luckiest family of Odessa. Many Soviet Jews or Seruvniks were ridiculed for years, harassed and prosecuted by the KGB as criminals, stripped of their human rights, their jobs, their homes, and some were incarcerated with murderers or ended up paying their last rubles to the Communist Party for "voluntarily" giving up their Russian citizenships.

Yep. Lucky us. But my cousin Devik remained Refusnik for another six years before they let him go to Israel. And when he finally arrived, it was too late for him to see my father Emil.

And it was too late for my Zeida.

LETTER TWENTY-FIVE: DOR HAMIDBAR

Zeida never made it to Israel, even after so many years of leading his small clan through the desert of oppressive Communist Russia. The term "Dor Hamidbar" is used to describe our ancestors who spent forty years in the wilderness before reaching the land of Israel. Alas, although they could see it from a distance, they could never reach it. For years Zeida led his family and friends through the darkness of Communist Russia, yet he was never permitted to reach the Promised Land.

LETTER TWENTY-SIX: PEARLS OF WISDOM

Zeida used many words and phrases I would not understand until much later. Like this one, for example: "Havel havalim amar Kohelet...." (Ecclesiastes 1:2). "Vanity of vanities, said Kohelet." And words like Singularity, Shekhina and others. Zeida often referred to Talmud, Tora, Kabala and Mishna, a compilation of ethics by the Rabbis from the period, also called Pirkei Avot, the Chapters of the Fathers.

Once Zeida said that Pirkei Avot is very unique because it is the only tractate of the Talmud to deal solely with ethical and moral principles. And on many occasions Zeida used this saying from Pirkei Avot 1:14 by Rabbi Hillel the Elder: "In ein ani li, mi li? U'kh'she'ani le'atzmi, mah ani? V'im lo 'akhshav, eimatai?" This translates to: "If I am not for myself, then who will be for me? And when I am for myself, then what am 'I'? And if not now, when?" I had no idea what he was talking about, yet it was all fascinating and strange.

It took a few years and a class or two in history to clear up a few things. I learned that Hillel the Elder was a famous Jewish religious leader born in Babylon who lived in Jerusalem during the time of King Herod. Hillel was one of the most important figures in Judaic history, and is associated with the Mishnah and the Talmud.

As you see, Zeida had a unique way with riddles and funny words, which he used to plant pearls of wisdom in my little head. But back then I was simply playing games with my cool grandpa Zeida. Once he transferred the number 770 right in front of my eyes to the silly word Parazta. And only during college while taking a class in theology did I understand this "magic": Number 770 was the address of "Our teacher's house," referring to the "Little Temple" at

the hopefully last exile of the Jewish People before they returned to Jerusalem to rebuild the Temple. And the name of "Our teacher's house" in every generation meant the dwelling of a current leader. As to the funny word Parazta, in Gematria (the Assyro-Babylonian system of numerology) it translates to "You will spread out." And surely Zeida also knew that 770 (on Eastern Parkway in Brooklyn) was the address of the World Headquarters for Chabad in New York City.

Zeida had many magic tricks up his sleeve, like turning the number eighteen into the Hebrew word Chai ("alive") and calling this a lucky number. Haa…, no wonder Miya always gave me eighteen chocolates, and Masha gave me eighteen Barbariska candies. Hmm…funny how things fit in so well at the end. Zakonomerno (naturally), as my mother Alla says.

LETTER TWENTY-SEVEN: TREE OF LIFE

A few articles were written in Odessa as well as in Jerusalem about Zeida, and some of them included photos. One old photo shows young men in dark suits seated by a table: the Odessa literary group. Seated with young Zeida are Frug, Bialik, Mendele Mocher Sforim and Shlomo Ansky, all renowned poets and writers.

There were also a few poems published. Here is one by Zeida's dear friend, poet Yohanan Giterman (1910-1991):

*There Was a Nice Man

In loving memory of a cherished man, Rabbi Meir Skulski (Zal"), Blessed his soul, who was my beloved friend and teacher, alav ha-shalom (rest in peace).

There was a nice man beyond the ordinary
His name was blessed upon our lips
Until my Lord added the name of "Zal"
Thus mourning and sigh were added too.

Forever remembered and blessed by our people
The name of this great man, great visionary
"The wisest of the clan" dwelled among us all
His eyes beamed with love and good heart.

In his sea of endless love we all willingly dived
Filled with desire to be immersed into the glow of his soul
Every Shabbat and Yom Tov (holy day),
We all gathered, drawn to him

There we spoke about Zion, living diaspora.
He conquered our hearts, his look filled with wisdom
His great wit, his brave Jewish heart
Each word, each idea as by glory of pearl

All drove our hearts closer and closer.
Remember, all the pupils, his teachings and ways
As none of you knew the readings of the Hebrew book back then,
But his endless patience for you all made it possible

Until you all became lovers of the Hebrew words too.
Great light discovered by you in deep darkness
A New World glared revealed to your eyes
Your hearts beamed desire for Holy

And love to your people and land of your ancestors.
And once you all arrived and gathered there,
In the blessed land, the Mother Land, Remember:
Do not sin! Praise with high arm

*The memory of **Nagid Haruach, ***Yad Vashem.*

*Translated by the author from Hebrew.
**1. Nagid was the most powerful representative of the Jews in the Middle Ages 2. Haruach means literally in Hebrew "the wind," Hashem.
***The idiom "Yad Vashem" taken from the Book of Isaiah: "…my walls place and a name (yad vashem) better than of sons and of daughters: I will give them an everlasting name, that shall not be cut off" (Isaiah 56:5).
"Tree of Life": In Chinese mythology the tree yields a peach every three thousand years, and it is guarded by a phoenix and a dragon; whoever eats the peach will live forever.

Part 2

LETTER TWENTY-EIGHT: TWO SUITCASES

It seems that after a year of harassing my family, the KGB got bored. After get my father Emil fired from his job they followed my family to Tolchok to make sure we would sell all we had, then they ran out of ideas and decided to get rid of us by signing visa papers. As I've told you, my family of four became the first family from Zeida's Ulpan allowed to leave Odessa, but the rest were all declined, and Grandma Polya, Miya and Devik remained back in Odessa. That is how the KGB operated, tearing families apart, harassing, squeezing the last ruble out of them, inflicting abuse, until the very last minute.

Once we got the visa each of us packed two suitcases in a hurry, preparing to leave behind family, friends and "Zhemchuzhina u morya," the pearl by the sea, Odessa...and looking forward to beginning a new life in Israel.

But how do you pack all your life into two suitcases?

My mother was leaving her friends and entire family behind. She also could not bring along her designer wardrobe, carved mahogany and white birch furniture and whatever was left from selling at Tolchok.

My father deliberated as to which of his books and paintings he could not part with as he frantically went through his fine collection of ancient Russian scripts. Turned out he would learn at the airport he had to leave them all right there to the greedy KGB agents anyway. All of his special-edition books and albums with coins and stamps from antiquity were confiscated as "The property of the Russian People" by a drunken, red-faced KGB bastard. None of it now belonged to my father, he said, since he was a traitor of the People. This, of course, was a bunch of crap coming from corrupted thieves in uniforms. My father Emil simply did not have any more rubles left for bribing the soldiers to look the other way.

Thieves!

Hooligans in uniform!

But isn't this just human nature? Seems there are always people who want to be free, as there are other people who oppress them with the same old methods. This is a simple equation. Just like in a big nasty sandbox with chubby babes fighting to win the brightest toy: Caesar, Napoleon, Mussolini, Hitler, Stalin, Khrushchev, Mao Zedong…they simply could not play nice in the sandbox.

So we packed our few belongings, fearing any moment the KGB might change their minds and announce they were just joking about letting us go. Sandbox cheating was commonplace in Soviet Russia.

My sister could not stop crying and complaining that her life would be forever ruined by leaving her friends behind, begging my father to let her stay in Odessa with Grandma Valya. But she was just frightened, especially after the KGB told us that once we left Odessa, we would never see our loved ones EVER AGAIN. I'm sure this was said by a red-faced agent as he smirked, barking the cold and dreadful words between his rotten teeth.

LETTER TWENTY-NINE: Departure: Aliya to Erez Israel

Many friends came to the Odessa Airport, remembering Zeida, excited and scared at once for our future in Israel, fearing for their own future in Odessa. They waved until we boarded the airplane.

The flight gave us our first taste of the capitalist lifestyle we could not get enough of. Instead of water we were served chilled Coca-Cola! An imperialist's drink, Stalin used to call this dark, sticky stuff. It was banned in Russia as a symbol of corrupted capitalism.

After flying a few hours drinking cola and snacking on Mozart truffles, we landed in a spotless airport with vast halls and elegantly dressed people. "Welcome to Vienna, Austria," the announcing voice proclaimed.

LETTER THIRTY: Austria

After a short bus ride we arrived at a magnificent palace out of the fairytales, but getting closer we saw it was surrounded by soldiers wearing black leather boots and metal helmets, and holding chained dogs. My mother immediately declined the palace, ready to run back to the airplane, but my father begged her to stay a few days, to enjoy living in a beautiful place in this once-in-a-lifetime opportunity, before boarding another plane to Israel. My poor mother kept clenching her teeth, squeezing my hand till my knuckles turned white, every time a soldier with a gray dog followed us. Were they protecting us, or afraid we might escape and get a job as many immigrants did? Who knows?

We stayed in Vienna only a few days, eating more Mozart chocolate, living in a marble palace, strolling the streets of civilized Vienna, until my father gave in to my mother's misery and we boarded an airplane for the second time that week for our final destination: Israel.

LETTER THIRTY-ONE: ARRIVAL

We spent the next day on a stuffy airplane packed with crying babies and sweaty people. When the plane landed and the engines finally quieted down and stinky gasoline vapors began to escape out the open door, I stared out my window, but there was nothing to see besides an empty field of sandy desert, and a dark sky illuminated only by beams of bright flood lights. "An airport!" my father proclaimed, smiling at my mother's horror. All around was sand and more sand; as far as I could see the sand was everywhere. In the distance a few white airplanes carried on their tails a picture of a star. "Look!" my father exclaimed, "Magen David, the Star of David!"

Once the door opened, my family squeezed out among the other passengers, all blinded at once by the glare of bright light and choking on hot air that reminded me of the heat from Aunt Miya's iron stove when we baked potatoes. We then walked down a funny metal ladder that resembled the one my grandpa Izya walked down to his basement to check on his pickles.

Reaching the ground, we were immediately surrounded by smiling men and women wearing funny sandals, white shirts, short pants and strange hats, like the ones Zeida used to make me from old newspapers. But the oddities did not cease there: The people with funny hats were all waving tiny flags with blue and white colors and a Star of David in the middle. Were they a bunch of local clowns greeting us? I wondered.

Then in the far distance appeared another strange scene: a small table on a wooden stage, same as the tables used by villagers at Tolchok to sell their livestock on. And why was the table covered with a plastic cloth? Even Grandma Polya had a better tablecloth for her table in Odessa. And as if all that was not strange enough, I saw very strange-looking people behind the table: A pirate-looking man with a black eye patch was seated with another old man who had a bunch of white wizard-like hair. And right in the middle of them both sat a lady dressed in a plain gray skirt and white shirt, her grayish hair styled in a bun.

My father gasped, then murmured in amazement:

"Oh my God...David ben Gurion [primary founder and first prime minister of Israel] and Moshe Dayan [the man with the eye patch and the Minister of Defense]...and...." My father's voice trembled and his eyes filled with tears. Why was he sad? Was he not supposed to be happy, finally arriving in Zeida's land? But just then, the lady started talking in a foreign language, followed by a Russian translation welcoming all to Israel, and my father exclaimed again: "Look at her, she looks like Babushka Polya!" And so right he was, to my amazement: Prime Minister Golda Meir, with her grayish hair and signature bun styled on her head, her strong profile and soft smile, her wrinkled face.... Amazingly, when I looked at her I could see my grandma Polya too! We all could. Wow! What an adventure.

Giggling to myself that same night as I began falling asleep in my new country, without remembering how I'd gotten into the bed, I looked forward to the next adventure, saddened for not being able to share everything with Miya, Devik and Babushka Polya, who were left back in Odessa. And it was too late for my Zeida.

After the welcoming ceremony at the Ben-Gurion International Airport in Israel, my father had been asked about the choice of our future residence. As both my parents were academics, our family was eligible to live for six months at an Ulpan run by Sohnut, an absorption department for newly arrived immigrants. Now my father had to choose the location of our Ulpan.

LETTER THIRTY-TWO: SDEROT

"Sderot is the nearest town to the center of Israel, Tel-Aviv," said the Sohnut agent. "Only about fifty miles away." Aha, sounds great, my father said, without thinking how FIFTY MILES without a car represents a very long distance. Something like walking from our house by the pond in New Jersey to New York City, and back home. Nevertheless, my family gladly went to Sderot as our new town. What did we know? All it meant, my father said, was that we were safe in Israel as free people. He was ecstatic to move into the small town of Sderot, completely oblivious to the fact that it was located in the southern point of Israel on the border with the Gaza Strip, and that its sky was sometimes decorated with occasional fireworks of Katyusha artillery (first built and fielded by the Soviet Union in World War II) launched from bordering Egypt by unhappy Hezbollah and other angry folks who did not play nice.

The very next morning, waking up in our new Sohnut apartment, we all ran outside to explore the area. Standing outside our new apartment building, we were taken by an unexpected mirage-like view: Everywhere we looked, as far as we could see, we were surrounded by sand, and more yellow sand!

I rubbed my eyes as even stranger images appeared in the distance: Two camels, a big one and one a little one, were walking with a man dressed in a funny white dress and wearing a strange white gauze on his head. The camels were held by a ring of black rope. The convoy was approaching my stunned family as the man kept waving both hands and yelling strange words at us. My mother grabbed our hands, ready to run away, as my father was ready to help save the stranger's life. Surely the poor guy was in trouble, he said.

We were standing in the sand, dressed up in our best outfits, as the stranger with the camels finally reached us, still yelling and waving both hands. Was the stranger a pirate, I wondered, kidnapping people to sell to a harem? (Miya used to read me *One Thousand and One Nights*.) As we stared at the old man's wrinkled face, locals translated his words and we were able to understand the intentions of this stranger. He was asking my father for a transaction: his big camel for my pretty sister—she was twelve—and the little camel for me, since I was only ten.

My astonished father thanked the stranger, politely replying that although he highly cherished the generous offer to sell his daughters to some Bedouin nomad Arabian clan, alas, the girls were not trained enough to fulfill the honor of becoming good wives, therefore my father must ensure proper training, and that requires time. We ran back home, laughing and glad to be alive; the stranger's dagger had been peeking out from under his belt. Was he a pirate? In the middle of a desert? Zeida never told us about such desert pirates of Israel. What an adventure it was! From then on it seemed anything was possible in Israel, except sharing it all with Zeida, Miya, Babushka Polya and Devik.

We spent six months at Ulpan Sderot to ease the process of absorption into our new land. After merely a few weeks, my father befriended local musicians and artists and my sister became surrounded by admirers young and old, as I resumed playing my violin and exploring the market with its local fruits and exotic nuts. Weekends were spent among friends, playing violin and visiting the neighboring Kibbutzim surrounding Sderot. Orange groves were part of an agriculture industry supporting several Kibbutzim in that area of the Gaza Strip.

One family practically adopted our family as they assisted us with the absorption process. Yehuda and Carmela Sagi lived in a nearby Kibbutz with two young daughters who were about the same age as my sister and me. What a wonderful family: They were warm, smart, kind, generous and fun-loving people. The father was a talented architect, Yehuda Sagi; the mother was a former student of famous violinist and conductor Yehudi Menuhin.

Carmela Sagi was an amazing and beautiful lady who became my first violin teacher in Israel, without charging my family the common fee. As the family lived on a Kibbutz, money had no value to them. Now it is all changed in Israeli Kibbutz. We were lucky as Carmela Sagi offered my family weekly free violin lessons for me. These generous people took my family under their wings of hospitality and treated me as a member of the Kibbutz, eligible to receive services that included a musical education. This was a lifesaver since there was no way my parents could afford my lessons back then. It was also the beginning of a life-long friendship between my family and the Sagis.

LETTER THIRTY-THREE: BROR HAYIL

Working day and night, my parents eventually saved enough for a down payment on a two-bedroom apartment in a new long pink building in Afridar, overlooking the green valley and the Mediterranean Sea.

During that time, a short bus drive took me to the neighboring Kibbutz called Bror Hayil for my weekly violin lessons with Carmela Sagi. The Kibbutz's name meant a "selection of soldiers" and was derived from associating with the Jewish revolt against the Romans in the first half of the second century. Besides that, there was a Jewish village by this same name during the Talmudic era.

A candlelight service at night in Bror Hayil Yeshiva—headed by Rabbi Yochanan ben Zakai—was a sign that a male child had been born. My lovely pedagogue Carmela Sagi said once that her Kibbutz was established on April 10, and I said "same as my father Emil," who was born on April 10. But that was the only resemblance: the Kibbutz was born in 1948; my father was born in 1937. And the Kibbutz remained alive long after my father was gone.

Did I tell you Carmela was a former student of

Yehudi Menuhin? His photographs were all around her studio. There were also photographs of Carmela's performances, including one photo of her playing on a stage with an orchestra conducted by Yehudi Menuhin.

Kibbutz Bror Hayil was located between Sderot and Ashkelon, where my family moved after our six months at the Ulpan. The entrance of the Kibbutz had a factory producing potato chips: Tapugan. Soon after purchasing our apartment, my father assumed a position of lead production engineer at the Tapugan factory, and I could see him there every week as I arrived for my violin lesson with Carmela Sagi. Although the Tapugan factory was situated on the Kibbutz premises, it was privately owned by the Swiss family of Gertrud Maser, her husband and two young girls who happened to live in Ashkelon, Afridar, in the same neighborhood in which we lived.

My weekly trips to Kibbutz Bror Hayil for violin classes with Carmela Sagi lasted three amazing years, and the mutual friendship between our families deepened during that time. My father was fascinated with Yehuda's work designing the streets and synagogues of Ashkelon, and my mother worked in his graphic design studio. Both our families enjoyed good company, music and trips around the country.

And during social gatherings, my father Emil was always the center of attention, telling jokes, playing piano, singing opera and making everyone feel very special and loved. And, as always, my kind and a bit shy but lovely mother was by his side, taking care of many requests with delicacies from her kitchen. Despite my parents' obviously different natures, they seemed to complement each other very well with their mutual respect, love and good friendship.

Also during that time I remember once performing with a chamber ensemble, the youngest musician playing as lead violin side by side with a lovely lady, Tzipora, our next-door neighbor in Afridar. She was in her fifties and told many stories about her young nephew, Gil Shaham, and his sister, Orli Shaham, who lived in America and performed at Carnegie Hall. Many years later I'd make the connection...as with many other events of my life, everything connected by circles. That boy, Gil Shaham, was born in Illinois while his parents, Israeli scientists, were on an academic fellowship there; his father Jacob was an astrophysicist, and his mother Meira Diskin was a cytogeneticist. Gil's sister is the pianist Orli Shaham. Gil graduated from the Horace Mann School in Riverdale, New York and, when he was nine years old, played for Isaac Stern! Later his teacher was Dorothy DeLay, also the teacher of many other leading musicians such as Itzhak Perlman, Sarah Chang and Jens Ellermann. The rest is history; Gil Shaham is a world-renowned violinist.

But I did not know all that back then. All I knew was that my neighbor Tzipora and her husband were a lovely, music-loving couple who once a week picked me up for a short half-hour drive to the nearby city of Ashdod to rehearse for about two hours. Tzipora and I often practiced violin together to prepare for the concerts we frequently performed at the local town hall.

LETTER THIRTY-FOUR: THE PINK BUILDING ON THE HILL

Situated on the hill by the Mediterranean city of Biblical Ashkelon, Afridar was named by South African settlers who established it in the mid '50s. From the pink building on the hill, right on the horizon you could see a thin strip of the Mediterranean Sea merging in perfect union with the greens of Hadeshe Hagadol, The Big Grass Park, creating a line of turquoise. And right below our windows down the valley, as far as you could see, there were orange crops that filled the apartment with the faint fragrance of the blossoms ascending from the valley. Looking at the green sea of trees below, I could not resist thinking of Zeida's reading: "…And the leaves of the tree are for the healing of the nations." (Revelation 22:1-22).

At horizon above the valley was a tower: the Mosque of Migdal or the Old Majdal Mosque, with its muezzin who awakened fellow Muslims for daily pray. Of course the muezzin woke me up every morning too, but at four o'clock I fell back asleep right away, fantasizing about sharing my many adventures with Grandmother Polya, Aunt Miya and cousin Devik, saddened by the notion we may never see them again.

There is a photo of my sister and me biting on oranges, dressed in pretty European silk dresses and lacquered boots from Italy. All dressed up, we are in the middle of the orange grove, where passing locals are dressed in t-shirts, shorts and sandals. Surely they thought we were a bunch of insane people from Mars. But we were quite oblivious to all that; soon after we moved into our new apartment, we all went down the hill to the valley, strolling with amazement in the maze of orange trees, enjoying their faintly fragrant and sweet fruits. The bees and wasps were buzzing all around as we enjoyed a taste of orange, biting one at a time with mixed emotions of joy and sadness that our Zeida did not live for this moment of celebration of life and freedom. Suddenly my father ran back to our apartment and returned with his camera. "Let's take a photo for Devik, Miya and Grandma Polya," he shouted eagerly. I told you already they were still back in Odessa, followed by the creepy KGB. And that was the first photo of my family's new beginning in our long pink building, which was as long as the fuzzy caterpillars of Odessa.

Haa…it is hard to explain to those living in America, where everything is available in abundance all the time. An orange, a banana and a bag of peanuts are all things you can get at every 7-Eleven or from any vendor on the streets of Manhattan, but in Odessa of the 1960s an orange had been a novelty less available than Beluga's caviar from the seaport.

LETTER THIRTY-FIVE: APPLE TREE

The following day I was wakened not by the mu-ezzin, but by the familiar whistle my father used to announce his arrival: the melody of the first bars from Tchaikovsky's Concerto #1 for Piano. Haaa, must be another cool adventure, I concluded, running to greet my father with my sister and mother. But rather than finding him with any type of anticipated surprise like a toy or maybe a new puppy to replace our puppy Dingo from Odessa, we found my father holding a tin can that contained a twig. "An apple tree," he said, and we all followed him outside, beneath our windows, to watch him place the twig in the ground. I had never had my own tree, and each day watering the twig, I would watch for any sign of a bud announcing a flower, and an apple.

Back in Odessa, Zeida once showed me a picture of a tree and said: "This is Etz Ha'Haim," Tree of Life. But all I saw were Hebrew letters with dots and crowns, almost like the musical notes for my violin, just funnier. I did not know back then that Tree of Life is a common term in Judaism for the Tora itself. Then Zeida showed me a small book with pretty colored pictures of a dragon and a funny-looking bird. "It is believed in Chinese mythology," Zeida said, "that the Tree of Life was guarded by a dragon and a bird called Phoenix…and once, every three thousand years, a sweet peach grows on that Tree of

Life, and whoever eats the fruit lives forever." Nice stories Zeida told me, but he never ate the fruit of the Tree of Life, and did not get to see Israel. Same as his son, my father Emil, did not eat the peach from the Tree of Life, and did not see the twig he planted grow into an apple tree.

LETTER THIRTY-SIX: GILDED STAGE

My parents' bedroom was not as big as the one I shared with my sister, yet it had a textured glass door leading to a lovely terrace overlooking the green valley with orange trees and the mosque. My sister and I shared a large bedroom with two windows overlooking both the valley beneath and a watch tower, the symbol of Afridar. Sharing my bedroom with my pretty sister carried many advantages and, well, responsibilities. Being admired by all, my sister had a line of admirers always knocking on our door, seeking her company. My poor sister tried in vain to get rid of her younger sister, who played the violin and wore thick round black glasses. But I was on a mission to be in the middle of all the action as much as possible, getting more creative each time. After a while, it got boring watching a line of popular teenagers covered with acne and long hair, smoking pipes and talking B-S, wearing sleeveless torn t-shirts exposing muscles…. Yep, I was jealous and did my best to stick around.

But after getting bored and tired of bothering my sister and her friends, I discovered that playing my violin in our adjacent small bathroom provided much better acoustic effects than in our room, and once the discovery was made, my daily practice took place in our bathroom. Our poor neighbors never complained. Looking at the mirror, I would imagine playing for Miya and Grandma Polya back on the stage of the Odessa Opera Theatre. I have a photo taken of me when I was about nine, playing on a gilded stage, Professor Mordkovitch in the background, Aunt Miya and Grandmother Polya in the audience.

LETTER THIRTY-SEVEN: PRETTY GIFTS

Our entire apartment was decorated with items my father collected during three years living in the pink building: antique daggers, silver blades and Roman swords were hung on the walls of the living room. Among the swords were canvas paintings my father painted, complemented by figurines depicting exotic antiquity battlefield scenes that were displayed on mahogany shelves along the wall. There were even a few mammoth ivory pieces my father had managed to get from Russia which were decorated with skillful seal-hunting engravings by the Inuits. And many other chachkies were lovingly displayed by my mother: an ebony elephant with ruby eyes, malachite plates, amber ashtrays, silver sculptures of Nefertiti....

As soon as you walked into our apartment you saw the tables, benches and shelves carved in fragrant sandalwood lining the walls, all standing on a wool carpet that covered the Israeli stone floor to help cushion us from outside noises. My mother's bedroom with its white dresser—a far cry from her white birch furniture of Odessa—was generously decorated with photos of family and many pretty chachkeis and other souvenirs with which my father showered her during seventeen years of marriage.

"Your daddy gave me a pretty gift every month for the first year of our marriage, and later on every anniversary," my mother said once. "Sometimes he spent all his money browsing in the antique stores of Odessa, searching for unique items. And once he found something special, he was excited as a child presenting me with his treasure." One of my favorites still is a small heart box complexly carved in solid ivory with patterns of delicate lace. As the box unlocks, a small white heart appears. My sister and I would sit and watch the heart turn green once the lights were turned off.

Among the many chachkies placed on the white dresser, there is also a black lacquered jewelry box dusted with gold powder and decorated with dragons and fuzzy mimosa blossoms.

LETTER THIRTY-EIGHT: KOLNOA RAHEL

My mother still lives in the long pink building, a complex of a few separate buildings, each with an individual entrance and all connected to each other by a wall. A vast complex shaped like a stretched letter M, it is made up of four-story buildings. The main entrance where my family lived is right behind the movie theater of Kolnoa Rahel, or Rachel Theater, which provided us with many cultural events to attend. The theater is fenced by a wall of bushes and, every spring just before Pesach, the hedge blossoms in clusters of fuzzy violet flowers that flood the air with their sweet fragrance.

Right across the street by the watch tower, small cafés and up-scale galleries merge with Hadeshe Hagadol. This vast green meadow of Afridar is a place to play soccer, bike and seek occasional relief from the scalding sun. Here you can sit on the benches under the eucalyptus trees and enjoy the breeze blowing from the nearby Mediterranean Sea. In one photo my smiling mother sits on a bench of Hadeshe Hagadol. My father took this photo in October, right before he was deployed to the Yom Kippur War in 1973.

LETTER THIRTY-NINE: KIPPUR WAR

A few weeks before my birthday, on an early morning of a sunny Saturday in October 1973, the quiet streets of Afridar were shaken by the distressed signals of sirens. Looking out the window, we saw an unusual scene, especially for Yom Kippur. Now, you need to understand that Yom Kippur, the holiest of holy days in Judaism, is observed throughout all of Israel by shutting down public transportation, movie theaters, restaurants, broadcasting stations...you get the idea. From the first star in the sky until next sundown, the entire country with solidarity respects the most holy day of atonement, mourning, reflection and redemption. And the only driving car you ever see in Israel during Yom Kippur is an ambulance, because saving Life is the holiest of mankind's missions, thus overriding observations of the holy Sabbath and the holiest Yom Kippur put together, as per our Tora.

All that being said, however, that Yom Kippur of October 1973 was unlike any other. The view outside my window was of complete chaos; of screaming, running people carrying yelling children; of cruising military jeeps loaded with men, some of whom had jumped out of bed still wearing their pajamas, others in Sabbath suits they'd worn to Synagogue. And now they were all off to defend their tiny Israel that was being cowardly attacked by surrounding Arab countries. Some sneaky bastards never play nice in a sandbox.

I cannot resist telling you about one of the myths out there: Since the U.N. voted for the establishment of Israel on May 15, 1947, the tiny state surrounded by unfriendly Arab countries has been portrayed by the world as a nasty aggressor that loves war and bloody fights. Well, look at the map: Israel, a tiny country the size of New Jersey, is almost encircled by powerful Arab countries that don't do a thing but stir up disharmony and confusion in the region, instead of.... Forgetaboutit.... I am trying to tell you that there is no other country in the world that longs for peace more than Israel, and that is one of the biggest lies you read. OK, that is it; just had to get it out of my system a bit. Makes me mad, all the lies and stupidity that lead to hatred of innocent people. Lastly, see for yourself what kind of "people" are using old women and young children as their shields while they fire on and kill other innocent civilians.

Emil Skulski in Sinai, Kippur War
Israel 1973

Now back to the Kippur War. As army jeeps cruised frantically along the streets of Afridar, soldiers yelling orders, men pouring from all the surrounding buildings, we saw my father Emil run outside among the first ones. We did not hear from him until October 23rd, when a loud knocking on the door startled us all and in walked an unshaven soldier, wearing a dusty uniform and a weary smile, who barely resembled my elegant and charming father who had left only a few weeks earlier. Per a special request, he had been granted a few hours to come home and wish me a happy birthday.

Postcard Emil Skulski sent from the Kippur War for Anushka's birthday October 1973

LETTER FORTY: ARIK SHARON

My father told us many stories about the Mitleh Mountains, the city of Ismailia and the Abu-Rodes oil field in Sinai, places with strange names that he went to during the war, but mainly he could not stop talking about a big man, a general named Arik, who came over to visit in the Mitleh Mountains and stayed all night with the soldiers, bringing them cigarettes and playing cards, explaining in perfect Russian to the division of mostly Russian immigrants the importance and crucial logistics of the next morning's battle!

Later on we all learned the big, gentle man had been Arik Sharon himself, who recently passed away after eight years in a coma. A great man was Arik, Ariel Sharon, admired and loved by so many people. I have a photo of my father Emil with Arik. They are smiling and smoking, wearing cowboy hats...later my father told us that most of the people in his group were killed in that battle, their chopped limbs scattered around the same place were only the night before they had played cards with Arik.

Shortly after his arrival home, my father Emil had to go back to the war. Just before he left, he took a photo with my mother. I carry this smiling photo on my keychain.... I also have another taken in the Suez Canal: It shows my father Emil sitting on a tank wearing a dusty uniform, smiling and so proud. Before returning to the war, my father gave me a large pendant made of solid gold and shaped as the Star of David, hanging on a long gold chain. I still have it! But I have no idea where he had the money for that expensive gift; most likely he sold some of his rare books, coins or stamps from years of collecting; he was a dedicated philologist. Father always managed with style and good humor. After a modest family celebration he returned to the front. In another photo from that day, my father is wearing his uniform and hugging my smiling mother. And here I have the postcard he sent just before his visit from the battlefield, wishing me a happy birthday. We used to laugh that the postcard arrived long after he came over.

LETTER FORTY-ONE: Hollow Ghost

After the war was finally over, my father returned home, celebrating our victory over a pack of cowards who had attacked us during the holiest of holy days. But the war was not over for my father, and it never left him. My father's behavior changed: There were no more sparks in his eyes, he no longer whistled the opening bars of a Tchaikovsky piano concerto before walking in, he did not play piano while singing "Ave Maria." Painting was the last to go.

My father's transformation was subtle yet profound. From a charming, charismatic man he turned into a different person, spending nights covered with blankets, as he had in the Sinai desert during the Kippur War, he said. He also began chain smoking, obviously reliving the horrors from the war, later telling my mother he could not bear the notion that he had not saved more of his soldier friends, after attending each funeral and seeing their severely broken bodies wrapped in white shrouds.

Post-Traumatic Stress Disorder became known only many years later, when Vietnam War veterans were finally diagnosed with it after so many years of suffering from the same strange symptoms. But it was too late to heal my father. And all my mother's love could not heal his wounds, and the horror of the war never left him.

LETTER FORTY-TWO: HAMSIN

Every April right before Pesach, gusty airstreams from the Sahara carry clouds of sand from the Egyptian border, covering Israel with a layer of dust. Windows are shut with specially designed trisim blinds in a vain attempt to keep sand from seeping indoors. During the Hamsin, dwellers of Ashkelon remain mostly indoors until the late evening hours, when the dust is swept away by breezes from the nearby Mediterranean Sea, allowing a temporary pause when it is possible to breathe outdoors without inhaling too much sand.

One day in April when I was fourteen, I returned home from school and, as usual, anticipated playing a game of chess with my father. He always won, of course, but I never gave up the challenge, mainly because I enjoyed his company. He no longer sang opera and played piano, yet I loved spending time with him very much.

But that particular day, my father left earlier than usual, without playing chess with me. He'd seemed a bit absent-minded, and all he said was "I will be back soon" as he left our apartment in Afridar.

I was the last person from my family to talk to my father. Growing up, I could never forgive myself for letting him go, and I became overwhelmed with guilt and pain. That was the last time any of us saw him awake and healthy.

Once someone said that my father left that day because he got bad news about one of his soldier friends from the Kippur War, but no details where ever found to support this. I will not write the rumors and the speculations about what happened that day, how maybe my father was attacked by someone who wanted to rob him of the money he'd managed to save with my mother. My father had big plans, but I do not have any evidence, just rumors and remarks I heard while growing up.

The next time I saw my father Emil, he was covered in white gauze, cocoon-like and lifeless as he lay in a coma at the ICU hospital of Ashkelon.

After ten days passed and my father still did not wake up, he began resembling an Egyptian mummy instead of a sleeping cocoon. Lying in an ICU bed by the breezy shore of the Mediterranean Sea, wrapped in white gauze from head to toe, his still body was interrupted by an occasional movement of the limbs. Just a neurological reaction, the fat doctor told my excited mother, as she waited for my father's full recovery. Was it just that, merely brain activity? Or was it his love of Life that made his heart fight, refusing to give up for so many days? But the doctor in a white robe followed by a fat nurse kept telling my poor mother the movements were nothing but a neurological reaction making muscles jerk; there was no brain activity. The doctor also said my mother was better off because my father would never wake up. If he did, he would spend the rest of his life impaired, in a vegetative state, and my mother would have to take care of his limp body; feeding, clean-ing...blah, blah, blah. My mother begged the doctor to do whatever it might take to bring my father back home to us; he loved Life and would do well in reha-bilitation, Mom said, and we would take care of him no matter what, she kept adding, begging in vain.

The fat nurse with her double-chin face looked shocked as my father's friends and my mother came over every day to visit my father and kept us from entering his room, barking orders to wait outside, to let him "rest," to stop disturbing him. Fat stupid cow.

Nowadays, it is a known fact that during a coma people need to be stimulated and many times they do come back. But as Russian emigrants used to complying with barking authoritative figures we quietly obeyed, waiting endlessly outside his room, not daring to do otherwise. Hm..., almost all of us.

Once I managed to sneak inside my father's room; I wanted to try to wake him up. I could not believe that my handsome, charming, charismatic, always smiling and happy father was so lifeless. And so I saw him for the last time, but before I could get a bit closer and touch him the fat nurse busted in, yelling and kicking me out.

My father passed away the very next day.

On April 16, 1975, Hamsin was at its peak, blazing across the land of Israel with a sea of sand. My eyes burned from the hot air. "Oh...Hamsin," proclaimed the locals, pointing to the clouds of sand wrapping around the cemetery.

The cemetery was in picturesque old Ashkelon with its synagogues, stone homes and a mosque, surrounded by orange trees overflowing with branches of sweet fruits like the orange trees in the valley below our two-bedroom apartment on the second floor of the long pink building in Afridar. My father's body, blanketed in a Jewish prayer shawl, was carried to the cemetery by Kadisha people, a burial committee. Staring at his body on the stretcher, I kept thinking maybe he would jump out of the shroud and proclaim this had all been one of his pranks; after all, just the other day I had seen him in the hospital, wrapped in gauze, thin tubes protruding in all directions delivering in and out colorful fluids that reminded me of the scarlet reds of poppies and the green shades of the hills behind our building in Cheromushki, Odessa. I could not wait to share all those thoughts with my father as soon as he woke up, when we would surely laugh about it all.

A sea of people were gathered by the gate of the cemetery, and the sun was right above our heads as the hot Hamsin air burned our eyes and lungs, drying our sweat and tears. We watched as the Kadisha people placed my father's body wrapped in its white shroud inside the ground (in Israel a coffin is avoided) on the back, as one who is going to sleep. Suddenly a very loud noise broke the silence: It was the body of my mother hitting the ground at the same moment the body of my father was placed inside his grave. A few people helped my mother to her feet; the rest screamed and cried. All but me.

On April 16, 1975, six days after his 38th birthday, my father Emil was buried under a clear sky, unlike the rainy day of Zeida's funeral back in Odessa.

At his gravesite, a white marble tower displayed an open book with lines of copper words from an Israeli lyric my father loved so much: "Et hamangina hazot i-efshar lehafsik…" This melody cannot be stopped.

There were so many people at the cemetery. All our friends from Odessa and Zeida's Ulpan, our new Israeli friends and neighbors, coworkers and us: my mother Alla, my sister Margalit with her boyfriend, Aunt Miya (there only for her brother's funeral) and me. Aunt Miya's son Devik was still in Odessa and Grandmother Polya could not find the strength to bury her third child. We were standing close to the grave; my mother had collapsed first while watching as the Tallit was wrapped around my father's body, then she fell the second time when the Kadisha people placed my father's body inside the grave as per Jewish tradition: dust to dust. My sister could not stop sobbing, tenderly held by her boyfriend, a young soldier who had came from IDF to pay his last respects.

Everyone cried but me; not even one tear squeezed from my wide-open eyes. I was stiff and cold, yet I could feel the stares of people who were probably thinking, "What kind of weird child does not cry for her father? Selfish, cold-hearted girl." But I did: in my way...away....

At fourteen, it seemed I had turned into a skill-ful builder, constructing a magnificent fort with a façade behind which my dark secrets lay. My father had been murdered and his killer remained free. All I was left with was the dream of killing the man who had taken my father's life.

That was that.

Charismatic and handsome, elegant and child-like, my father had managed to charm an iron fist of bureaucrats and clerks within the Russian Com-munist Party, always getting his way with authorities and pretty girls, but in Israel he met one bureaucrat he was not able to charm away: a bureaucrat named Grim Reaper.

LETTER FORTY-THREE: Rakefet

After that, we tried to make the best out of Life; we continued to study, work and laugh, just as my father Emil would have liked us to do. My sister got married to her soldier boyfriend and I met your dad at a Hanukah party with mutual friends. I was sixteen and he was twenty-four. We dated for a few years and, after a modest wedding, your daddy and I purchased a studio by the beach of the Mediterranean Sea.

It was on Rakefet Street, within walking distance of the long pink building where my mother still lives. Many friends and family were always welcome in our cozy studio with its garden by the beach. Eventually we would welcome there Grandpa Izya, Grandma Valya, Aunt Bebah with her family, Aunt Miya with little Erez (Devik's son), and others such as Lyona Shultz from Zeida's Ulpan and Grandma Elizabeth, your father's mom. They were always welcome for a cup of freshly brewed coffee or a barbecue your dad gladly served in the garden.

Enjoying good company and great food, we all gathered around a table under a tree in the middle of the yard. The meals were plain yet skillfully orchestrated by your dad, who loved to put on a gourmet performance, to our amusement and satisfaction. Your dad had a reputation as a man of many skills.

LETTER FORTY-FOUR: VISITING MY MOTHER BEFORE AMERICA

To reach my mother's building, carved into the north side of the scenic hills of Afridar, we would weave through narrow streets filled with peach and guava trees. I made this journey almost daily, back and forth from Mom's building to the studio on Rakefet Street. Each time I visited my mom her table was loaded with plates filled with baked goods, salads, fish. She would insist that anyone who visited have a bit of this and that, and would keep pouring more of this and that, lastly serving her famous chocolate cake with coconut and frosting, plus a generous layer of scarlet preserved cherries.

This time my visit had not much different than others, and the smell of coffee that usually preceded my departure did not prepare me for what happened next. "Fergana...," my mother dreamily said, as if answering a question. She had been behaving in such a way lately and although it worried me, I'd learned there was usually a purpose to her dream-like remarks.

"Thanks for the coffee," I said, watching her pour another cup of coffee for both of us. This time it was her signature cup of espresso café topped by the fluffy froth of steamed cream. Mom also placed another slice of cake on my plate. "Eat, eat, you look skinny," she said, obviously not ready yet for my departure.

"Your grandpa Izya (Israil Davidovich Berdichevski) was not the same man after Danya was killed," Mom then said. Hmm...surely she knew I remembered Uncle Danya, her baby brother, who was killed in the army at the age of nineteen, survived by his new wife and newborn baby boy, Arthur. I recall my Uncle Danya as a young tall man with a knotty smile and wide shoulders, always bringing over a gift of a toy or a doll for my sister and me.

"My father Izya and your daddy Emil," Mom continued, "had become very good friends and decided to work together; they established an entire enterprise at Kolkhoz, a collective farm. They'd envisioned my brother Danya as part of that family enterprise.... But Danya's destiny was about to change. He had turned eighteen when he met a gorgeous girl with long hair and mysterious green eyes, Nadia. Turning nineteen, he received the mandatory letter stating he was being drafted into the Red Army; three years of going away, not like nowadays, when service people can visit on vacations and weekends.... In the Russian army you were gone three years, and many Jewish boys never returned home. Danya married his sweetheart, who carried his child. He was nineteen, she was eighteen.

"When Nadia delivered a baby boy, Danya requested to be granted special permission to visit his new bride and newborn son. But the Russian army had a strict policy of mandatory service of three full years, without any visitation. Once deployed, you were gone for three years.

"Danya, terribly missing his wife and newborn son, decided to figure out a way back home, but he was hit by a military car…. He was nineteen.

"…and Yuzic died too shortly after…," my mother continued. Of course I remembered my Uncle Yuzic: Tall and skinny in his late twenties, he was married to my mother's youngest sister, Bebah, and died at twenty-eight of kidney cancer, but mainly because of the Communist bastards. You heard me right, no typos. And that is why I tell you this now.

Bebah was pretty and blond and not yet seventeen when Yuzic, Josef Lisman, fell madly in love with her while serving in the army. Yuzic had sky-blue eyes and a black mane of shiny hair. To everyone's amazement, he was released before the end of his army term by almost two years, but he had to wait for Bebah to turn seventeen before they could marry. The newlywed couple enjoyed a wonderful loving marriage and had two daughters: Zina and Ella; yep, my cute cousins.

Seemingly all was going well for the family: working, raising little girls…. I remember my Uncle Yuzic never complained and worked very hard to provide for his lovely family. After his second daughter, Ella, was born he didn't feel well and went to see a doctor. But that was already too late. The doctor made all the tests and finally exclaimed in horror: Where were you until now, never visiting for a checkup?!

This is what happened: Everyone has heard

about the Russian space program (and I am not under chemo brain right now, so please keep reading to see how it is all connected). They were the first to send a satellite to space with a cosmonaut, Yuri Gagarin, on board. Right? But not too many people know about the second satellite the Russians launched, this time with a cosmonaut named Titov. Apparently Uncle Yuzic served in a special division that worked on that project, and his entire division was present in a space aerodrome the day the second Russian satellite was launched into space.

Shortly after, Yuzic with his entire division didn't feel well…without further explanation or doctor examination, his whole division was immediately dismissed from the Red Army, followed by a modest pension and the medal of a Red Star, the highest honor. Can you imagine how happy young Yuzic was? To be dismissed early from the army? To go back home, get his life back? And so he did. He went home, got married, had two beautiful daughters….

After the doctor explained his test results, Yuzic just replied: "My mother died at twenty-eight during labor (he was raised by his father), so will I die too at twenty-eight." Yuzic was at once hospitalized in the oncology department, where his doctors thoroughly explained his situation: He had been exposed to a huge amount of radiation, level 90, which was now resulting in kidney failure and cancer…. He had only a few weeks left to live.

And just as the doctor said, Yuzic died, leaving behind his devastated wife with two little girls, the oldest four years old and the youngest just two months old.

"My father Izya buried Yuzic in the Odessa cemetery, in the same plot of his mother Dora and son Danya (David Berdichevski)," my mother said.

But my mother surely knew I remembered my great-grandma Dora, Uncle Yuzic and Danya. There was something else. But what? "But a long time ago," my mother continued after a short pause, "before Yuzic and my Danya, when I was three years old, during World War II, we all evacuated from Odessa to Asia, and there was another baby…baby boy…," my mom said, looking over my head. "Fergana," she added, saying nothing more as she cleared the table of our empty plates and cups.

Though curious about all that had happened, especially the last "Fergana" word, I was glad to go back to my little studio by the beach, excited to keep packing for the trip your father and I were about to take to London and New York City.

To America

Part 3

LETTER FORTY-FIVE: WHERE ARE YOU FROM?

"So why did you come here?" curious folks kept asking me in America, immediately recognizing a trace of a foreign accent slipping through my English. "Where are you from?" they constantly questioned, as though insisting on attaching to me a tag with some sort of definition (or perhaps attempting to make sense of their own? Seems we all try to make sense by organizing things into labeled boxes.).

Some folks insisted I must be from Brazil with such a soft accent. "Sounds just like Portuguese," they said. Others claimed I look like a French lady, and occasionally few would recognize my underlying accents: a trace of Russian layered with coarse Hebrew consonants. After all, in Odessa I was The Jew, in Israel the locals defined me as Hanna the Russian, and once I came to live in America most people claimed I must be an Israeli. To add a bit more confusion, my father Emil had changed our last name of Skulski to Meir shortly after our arrival in Israel. Yes, for Zeida's name. And with all that said, my initial irritation changed with time to amusement morphing to boredom, forcing me to come up with some lame excuse.

But to you I now tell this: Your dad and I decided to take a break from the chaotic life of the Middle East conflict: daily Katyusha rockets killing civilians and destroying people's homes, the country paralyzed with the horror of bodies severed by suicide bombers who blew up buses carrying little children out of a fundamental quest to accent Heaven with pretty virgins. We decided to leave it all behind just for a while, before losing our cools, and to go on an adventure and travel without worries. And first we went to London, where we browsed in museums and in Trafalgar Square, and then we went to visit New York City.

LETTER FORTY-SIX: YOUR DAD

Young and old people all over the world dream of America, the land of endless opportunities and freedom. So did your dad, but with plans that differed a bit from mine. Let me try to explain.

Your grandfather on your father's side was born in Hungary in the Satmar region, the birthplace of the Hasidic dynasty. Your dad was born in Targu Mures into an ethnic Hungarian family that had lost most of its ancestors to the horrors of Auschwitz, to be replaced after the war by even worse tortures by the Russians. Communist Russia decided to "relocate" Romanian farmers among the national Hungarians, renaming the land as Romania and the region as Transylvania.

Like other Hungarian children of the region, your daddy and his oldest brother Tomy spoke the Hungarian language at home until they both attended school, where they were forced to speak the Romanian language, and later on to learn mandatory

Russian.

Your daddy's mother Elizabeth lost her parents and six siblings during the war; his father Samuel lost his first wife Eva and firstborn son Tomy in Auschwitz, where he later met Elizabeth. After the war, the couple found courage to start anew. They married, had two boys—your daddy and uncle Tomy— and moved into a small house with a garden. Samuel bought a grocery store and worked there from dawn to dusk in order to provide for his little family's needs.

The family often visited relatives in Budapest to share memories and new hopes, until one day when they were gone the Russians confiscated their lovely house for some high-rank general, followed by the second blow: the Russians confiscated their tiny grocery store for The People; no private property was allowed in Communist Transylvania.

Devastated and heartbroken, the family patriarch Samuel was from then on an employee for The People, the Party, often selling to the pretty wife of the Russian general who now lived in his house. It was only a matter of time before bottled-up agony erupted and Samuel had a stroke and died, leaving behind Elizabeth and their sons: Tomy was twenty, your daddy was sixteen.

Losing all they had, the devastated family left the ruins of their life behind and immigrated to Israel to begin a new Life. Elizabeth had to learn job skills, how to sew and work in local factories. The boys pitched in and assumed odd jobs, later serving in the IDF. Young men had a mandatory service of three years in the Israeli Defense Forces; women had to serve for two years. While helping to protect their new land from so many terrorist attacks and wars, the family kept struggling as new immigrants, never losing hope.

When your dad served in the Israeli Defense Forces he fought in the 1973 Yom Kippur War just as my father Emil, though they never met. Your dad also fought during the 1982 Lebanon War against Arafat's terrorists.

When I met your daddy in Israel, at the Hanukah party of a mutual friend, he obviously had had enough of the political arena of Israel, and I was ready for an adventure. After we married we planned to go to London and travel to New York City. That is how your daddy and I arrived in America as a young couple looking for a break and a worry-free visit to this vast country, and each time we visited a new place we were filled with awe for this magnificent land, as well as peace of mind. Eventually we decided to stay, and your daddy built a good career and I gladly watched this quiet and somewhat reserved man thrive and reinvent himself, far away from the endless Israeli-Arab conflict. To America

After all, America has long been a world magnet with well known slogans such as "The sky is the limit," "Land of endless opportunities," "Be the best you can be." But as I tell you and your sister all the time, living in America is not that easy of a task because it comes with the huge responsibilities of freedom, the need to choose to either become your own very best self, or to become absolutely nothing. That is the price tag attached to any free society.

LETTER FORTY-SEVEN: TEMPORARY UTOPIA

"And what about you?" you may wonder. "Why did you leave Israel after all the troubles your own family endured in Russia in order to immigrate to Israel to begin with?" Hm...that is a good question, but as you know I do not have short answers, although I could flatly reply that America is a great country, a land of opportunities...blah blah blah.... But if you really wish to know and still keep reading, I would say just this: America seemed a place of temporary Utopia, where the ghosts from the past may vanish for a while. An emotional Band-Aid, if you will. But as you know, more than once a Temporary turns into the Permanent, like a piece of furniture purchased to just fill in for a while that eventually turns into something you have for the rest of your life. You know what I mean? Something like that.

LETTER FORTY-EIGHT: AMERICA

Our first dwelling in America was a two-bedroom rental in a massive Victorian home right behind Brooklyn College that was occupied by another young couple while the owner resided on the upper floor. Easy access to college allowed me to resume studies in psychology, education and art, as well as to

befriend wonderful people. Mostly I recall my English teacher, Professor Pandora, a lovely lady in her
late forties who conducted summer concerts on her
lawn by the Atlantic Ocean. I have one photo of a
semi-circle of seated musicians and in the center is a
very pretty lady wearing a long dress and pearls, and
next to her is me, playing the violin.

One of the other people I befriended was Aunt
Ida.

LETTER FORTY-NINE: IDA

Before I left Israel, my mother insisted that I
pay a family visit to her Aunt Ida in Brooklyn. And
as soon as I met Aunt Ida in her apartment by the
Atlantic Ocean on Brighton Beach, she showed me
photos of her late husband who was killed during
World War II, young and handsome Grisha, Grandma Valya's brother and my mother's uncle. A photo
of Aunt Ida shows a lady in her late eighties, with a
smooth porcelain complexion, hazel eyes, short gray
hair and a warm smile.

Aunt Ida's two-bedroom apartment in a red
brick building of Brighton Beach was not far from
neighboring Sheepshead Bay, where your daddy and
I soon purchased our first home in America. We had
figured out that renting was not the wisest thing to
do for the long-term as we were paying someone
else's mortgage. So we both worked two jobs around
the clock to save for a down payment to buy a house;
we even used to rent our walk-in basement for a

while to pay off monthly bills.

Visiting Aunt Ida, who was merely a few minutes away from our house, was always a pleasant event. Even before entering her modest apartment, I was struck by the familiar fragrance of Grandma Valya's kitchen. Seems the entire Jewish community back in Odessa of my childhood had cooked the same exact way. The aroma of Aunt Ida's apartment was detected way before I reached her wide-open door to see her with her warm smile, and receive from her a hearty hug.

The walls of her living room were generously covered with photos layered on top of barely noticeable fading wallpaper. In the epicenter of the high ceiling was a porcelain chandelier decorated with gilded flowers that seemed oddly out of place in the modest apartment. Aunt Ida once said that kitschy thing was actually her favorite item, simply because it was the last gift from her daughter, pretty Dorochka, whose photos were displayed among others.

Dorochka was gorgeous before breast cancer ate her flesh away just one year before I met Aunt Ida. And it seemed as though Destiny played a prank, because a month or so after I met Ida, I was diagnosed with breast cancer too. Coincidence...or another circle of Life?

The small apartment on the second floor across from the ocean always smelled like Odessa. Aunt Ida had an abundance of pots, plates and jars ready to serve guests with homemade Forshmak, Golubzi, Selodochka and other traditional dishes from the Jewish culinary circles of Odessa. In addition to the selection of such dishes, I never got tired of the flow of her tales. I listened once again to the story of my grandpa Izya saving her life and those of her three little children (Dorochka, Sasha/Alex and Pavel) during World War II; about the loss of her husband during the war and how she struggled as a single mother to raise three kids after the War.... Many tales were told in her apartment, each more fascinating than the previous one. We spent evenings remembering, eating and talking. Aunt Ida had so many stories to share, and I enjoyed listening to them all.

Aunt Ida was a lady. Modest and humble, she was a brave and wise matriarch who was cherished, loved and respected, especially by those who knew she had raised alone three children in the profound poverty of the post-war era. My mom once said Aunt Ida rejected many advances from a line of admirers. She was very pretty in her youth, Mom said, yet selflessly dedicated to raising her children.

One photo of Aunt Ida shows her standing by a lady with red hair and green cat-eyes, her sister Shelly. Both had magnificent grace, smooth white complexions and beautiful cat-like eyes; while Shelly had a gorgeous crown of red hair, Aunt Ida had rich chestnut hair. Mom said people always used to stare at them both.

Each time her sister Shelly visited from San

Francisco, Aunt Ida phoned me to come over, and the three of us would enjoy hot red cabbage soup topped with cold fresh sour cream, and lovely conversations.

Hm...I have so many nice photos to share, like one of smiling Aunt Ida surrounded by family. It was taken in the Odessa restaurant, where we celebrated her ninetieth birthday.... And this one is of my mother and sister, who came over all the way from Israel, where they both reside, for the party.... And this photo shows Aunt Ida and me; I'm wearing a pink shirt that hung on my bony shoulders. I was having weekly chemotherapy treatments and wore that blouse after you seemed to be embarrassed of your bold mom, and annoyed when people stared at me. You were only six and nine, and I did my best to look normal for my babies. Remember how we all laughed when you drew my eyebrows and lashes that had fallen off? "I will paint you," you said and seems you both were great artists, since people did not stare at me too much.

LETTER FIFTY: DORA

Last time I visited Aunt Ida, she warmly greeted me as always: "Lubonka...." Lovey. It was May 9th, and as I'd done every year since we met, I had stopped by to celebrate Den Velikoy Pobedu, Day of Great Heroic Victory, the end of World War II (May 9, 1945), with her. We each had a small flute of Manischewitz, her favorite sugary wine, to commemorate Russia's sweet victory over the German Nazis. And, as usual, Aunt Ida had her photo album open on the kitchen table, and told me old stories I loved to hear all over again.

Aunt Ida was a great storyteller with a soft pleasant voice, yet some people said "She talks too much... Nudnik...." But I didn't mind at all. I was fascinated by her tales, especially since she was a link to my mother's family. The flow of her tales was paused only by her bringing in new plates of delicacies. I heard again about her husband who never returned from war; the uncle and son who went to fight the Germans, leaving behind their wives and children, hopeful that civilized Germans, once they occupied Odessa, would not harm the weak and helpless civilians. At that point Aunt Ida used to pause for the longest time, before repeating the story of Grandpa Izya's mother Dora.

"Your grandpa Izya's mother's name was Dora Izrailevna Berdechevskaya," Aunt Ida said. "She was a clever lady who decided to flee Odessa, unlike many wives and children of the soldiers. She did not have much trust in Civilized Germans to spare the innocent civilians, and she left Odessa way before we all were evacuated to the Fergana Valley." As Aunt Ida said this I stared at her in astonishment; it was the first time she had mentioned this name, as my mother had back in Israel on my last visit before arriving in America. But I did not want to interrupt the flow of her thoughts.

"She carried one suitcase," Aunt Ida continued.

"Dora left the shores of the only place she ever knew—her beloved Odessa—with the first available boat, after failing to convince her family to join her. That day her two sisters stayed at home to cater to the young and the ill, including their sick father, and asked the oldest child, Genya, to accompany Dora to her departure. After hugs and waves, Dora departed, waving goodbye to her lovely niece Genya.... That was the last time Dora ever saw her."

No matter how many times I hear this story, each time my heart sinks anew, as though I'm hearing the story for the very first time. And now I will tell it to you so you can see for yourselves why.

Great-grandmother Dora, my grandpa Izya's mother, had two married sisters and they all lived in a lovely building located on 114 Kirov Street, which was lined with acacia trees. When World War II began, the strong and young left Odessa to fight the invading Nazis and protect their beloved Odessa. The rest remained back at home: the old and the sick, women and children. Among them was my grandmother Dora's entire family. Genya was the oldest of the children and the family summoned her to escort Dora to the seaport. After waving goodbye to the departing boat carrying her aunt Dora, Genya hurried back home.

Shortly after Dora's departure, the German soldiers marched into Odessa yelling "Outen" in German, ordering frightened civilians to gather on the streets. And once people left their homes, obeying the invaders, the first thing the Germans did was to shoot the old and the ill. Crying babies followed, and then their hysterical mothers. Then the Gypsies, the ugly, the invalids…, but many were spared, mostly young Jewish men and women. You heard me right. At first, people thought the horrors of the Jewish people being systematically exterminated must have been just a crazy myth; surely civilized Germans, Wagner music lovers, would never reach to that low of a human scale….

The young men and women were surprised when the German soldiers ordered them to the trucks instead of shooting them in the head. They all gladly climbed in, like a heard of sheep, leaving behind only a few women. How could they know the trucks would take them to the concentration camps for labor and starvation followed by death in the gas chambers, all part of the Third Reich's Final Solution? But the destiny of a few women left behind on the streets of Odessa was no better; and Genya was among them. Pretty eighteen-year-old Genya was spared the camp to be later raped by soldiers in front of her sick father…. Then the soldiers shot Genya in the head and hanged her lifeless body on an acacia tree, across from the house in which her family lived…. As Genya's body was hanging, the German soldiers loaded what remained of her family into the trucks, and took them away to the concentration camps.

But Dora could not know all that when her ship departed Odessa's shore while Genya waved goodbye on the pier.

"Dora was a gifted tailor," Aunt Ida said, "who crafted complex patterns of clothing, but her life was not crafted as well. When her husband David Berdichevski reached the age at which all young Russian males had to serve mandatory terms of three years in the Red Army, he was told by family and friends about a great way to avoid the draft: All he had to do, right before the medical exam for the army, was to drink plenty of strong black tea to trigger an irregular heartbeat so he would be excused as unfit to serve. Ha…. Smart, right?

You see what happened, though: He drank a lot of strong tea, each year, each time, right before the medical exam. And each time he was found unfit to serve. "A weak heart," the doctors said. As time went by and he kept avoiding being drafted, David married Dora and their two sons were born: Israel Davidovich (your grandpa Izya), followed by his little brother Zahar Davidovich. Look at this photo of a tall handsome man holding a young boy next to a seated, smiling lady with a toddler. The young couple, David and Dora, took care of their little boys as David kept drinking his strong black tea, successfully avoiding being drafted. All went well until one day he got very ill, and the doctor said, 'Too much of the black tea has ruined your heart and done irreversible damage.' David became weak and was eventually unable to leave his bed. Dora assumed a job at the factory, caring for her sick husband and two little boys.

"David was thirty-seven years old when he died

of heart failure, leaving behind devastated Dora and two little boys aged seven (Izya), and four (Zahar). Zahar one day would be sent to the Siberian Gulags…but that is another story. And also remind me to tell you about Fergana," Ida concluded. Ha, again this word my mom had mentioned back in Israel….

And that is the story Aunt Ida told me once again on the day I stopped by to celebrate Den Velikoy Pobedu. I made a mental note to ask her about Zahar and Fergana on a future visit, but in the winter of 2002, Aunt Ida passed away.

LETTER FIFTY-ONE: LITTLE GEORGE AND OLD GEORGE

Living by the bay, your daddy and I enjoyed the daily catch offered by local fishermen. A photo shows our house, connected in a long row to identical red brick homes of Sheepshead Bay, a diverse and dense place populated by Russian stores, Chinese bazaars, Indian restaurants and other ethnic joints.

Our neighbors' yards were manicured by Italian families and pragmatically vegetated by Chinese families who grew fresh produce, wisely dividing their small backyards into rows of vegetables and fruits. Unlike the sophisticated yards of our neighbors, our backyard was simply a place to play, to swing and to chase our crazy chocolate Labrador. Once in a while, between work, college classes and errands, I planted tomatoes and strawberries to show you and your sister that fresh foods do not grow inside supermarkets. Remember eating fresh tomatoes and strawberries right from the stem? We have photos of your little faces smeared with tomato juice taken under the disapproving stares of our neighbors.

Our block was a very busy place, to say the least, full of traffic from ambulances, garbage trucks, taxis, buses, cars…. And after our neighbor to the right—Old George—died, a Chinese family moved in with a little boy named…George. Besides growing fresh produce, they also rented their basement to relatives; your daddy could not stop complaining that our place smelled like Chinese take-out.

One photo shows the family's youngest child, Little George, his tiny body covered with scabs from constant scratching; the poor thing was allergic to anything and everything from dust to eggs. Another photo shows you and Little George standing on our deck, both the same size, although you were two and he was seven. Yep, that is how tiny Little George was, or Georgie as everyone called him. A nice and polite boy that Little George was. Poor thing; I hope he is better these days despite his allergies and eczema and who knows what else.

I liked our new neighbors with Little Georgie; they were nice, hard-working people. The mother was always cooking, cleaning or sewing on her machine as the father worked long hours at construction. She always had a plate for me with a Chinese delicacy, and I gladly shared the strawberries and tomatoes from my garden. That is how it was: good neighbors without a word in English. Nice family, good people.

LETTER FIFTY-TWO: OLD NEIGHBOR GEORGE

But before the Chinese family with Little George moved next door, Old George lived there. I know, you do not remember, and how could you? You were only eight months when he passed. Old George was a wrinkled man in his late nineties who carried his bent-over body on a pair of bowed legs. He came from a family of Klezmer, Yiddish-speaking Jewish musicians who arrived in America between 1880 and 1924. Old George always had a story and a song to share, until one day he pointed down his bony thumb and said, "Anna, no more singing, but sinking." And since that day, every time we met, he would greet me with a song, pointing down with his thumb, with a wink and a soft whisper at the end: "I am still sinG-ing, but with the K."

Old George was a funny man, but soon after I saw a middle-aged lady at his home who insisted on feeding George with a few spoons of soup. But Old George had made up his mind and refused all attempts to sustain his weakened body with food or any other treatments that might heal his newly diagnosed stomach cancer.

The day I came to say goodbye, carrying you in my arms, I saw his lean shape had gotten impossibly thinner as he lay sunken under white linens in his dark bedroom. And that was the last time I saw Old

George. Some people said it may be bad luck for me and my little boy to visit a dying man; people are so silly. I simply came to say Goodbye.

LETTER FIFTY-THREE: CIRCLES OF LIFE

Once you and your sister reached school age, your daddy and I decided it was time to move to the suburbs in order to provide you with a better education and a safe place to grow up. We moved to a small colonial surrounded by ponds and brooks, about twenty minutes driving distance from New York City. It was an easy commute to work and to the museums and galleries I frequently visited with you both.

Shortly after we moved to the suburbs, I was given a pink tote bag. Inside the bag, among pink candies and a winged angel pin with a fake pink diamond, was also a letter saying Breast Cancer... stage*^%.... I did not read the rest, just blinked at the pair of pink ribbon shoelaces in the tote bag. The candies and the pin were supposed to comfort me as I stared at the letter, drifting away and thinking, Why would somebody give away a pair of shoelaces to a newly diagnosed cancer patient? A lady seated next to me seemed to have similar thoughts as our eyes locked and we both faintly smiled.

At that same crazy moment, a light bulb went off in my head: Surely I could make a cool item better than a pair of shoelaces...and that crazy moment turned into the birth of my business, which kept me

sane during my treatments. I would design innovative and neat items made from recycled pink glass to
replace the pair of shoelaces in the gift bag, as well
as to replace my fear, anger and burning desire to
fight my MF#$%SOB$%# cancer. What choice did
I have? You were only nine years old and your sister
was six; I had to be around for a bit longer.

After cycles of chemotherapy, radiation treatments and other stuff I had to go along with in order to get rid of crappy cells in my body, I angered
my doctors by declining the protocol of follow-up
treatments with group therapy and physical therapy.
Group support was way too depressing, and physical
therapy was conducted by newly graduated, cheer-
ful, chubby-cheeked young people who would flock
eagerly to my side with chirps of "What a wonderful
day!" despite my clearly visible post-surgical discom-
fort and the fact I was walking around with protruding tubes and a bag of yucky drainage.

To save whatever was left of my sanity, I switched
a doctor or two, started playing tennis with a bunch
of great ladies—all cancer survivors with the organization Tennis For Life—and decided to substitute
boring physical therapy with learning to sculpt in
rock with new friends Natalie Frier and Ulla Novina. It was not as easy as I thought, and was really
tough at the beginning, but eventually it proved to
be a great way for me to strengthen my arms and
clear my chemo-brain from its foggy blanket. But
rigorous sculpting in rock did not do much to clear
the depression I fell in.

LETTER FIFTY-FOUR: DEAREST GEORGE

As my healing with arts kept evolving, many strangely amazing things began to happened. All of a sudden a short documentary about my healing called The Art of Healing was aired on cable TV, and an art exhibition in New York City was followed by another exhibition at the Art Museum of Queens. This was all followed, however, by my sinking into a deep depression from being on Tamoxifen, as well as being in a hurry to swallow all that there was, exhausting my already depleted stores of energy.

My doctor dismissed my depression as a direct result of the Tamoxifen and insisted on anti-depressants, and all I could think of was the zombie effects experienced by PTSD veterans I'd worked with in Israel. Declining anti-depressants and ditching the doc, I met Dearest George. Dearest George saved me from myself right before he passed away from ALS, exactly as he'd said he would when we first met at his Teaneck studio three months earlier. The hardest part during our weekly sessions was watching Dearest George slowly lose his balance until he ended up on crutches, his supportive wife by his side, and eventually lost his ability to speak.

Dearest George (blessed of memory), Dr. George Greenberg, was a renowned psychotherapist from a long line of great Rabbis. He was a wise scholar with a kind soul, who is profoundly missed by all; blessed be his memory.

LETTER FIFTY-FIVE: THE GIRLS WITH AMAZON HEARTS

And then I met the Amazon Girls; albeit all the credit goes to Dearest George, my therapist Dr. Greenberg (Zal"), who empowered me to go back to do the one thing I knew well how to do: reinvent myself anew.

You know, motorcycles always scared me a bit, the idea of losing control and crashing my bones, yet at the same time I have been fascinated by bikers with their free spirits, ready to take off and fly away. But that was all it was; nothing but an illusion or an impression without any substantial intention of ever riding a motorcycle. It was never on my mind and way out of my timid comfort zone. But then all that changed. After losing many friends to cancer and after my Dear George died too, that was exactly the one thing on my mind: What could be better than the sweet revenge of teasing Mr. Grim and celebrating Life by overcoming my fears, one by one? Surely Dear George would agree with me.

And that was the beginning of my new, once-in-a-lifetime adventure to reinvent myself once again: a journey that left fears behind and created new friendships with people from all over the world, each different than another yet all with the same passion and love of Life, all of whom had survived breast cancer and wanted to do what they liked most: ride

Harley-Davidsons, and help others beat cancer.

It seemed we all had to brush off traces of chemo brain and stop being numb with fear and following a way we all knew too well. We had to dive in head first and ride up the ridge coast of California, from Los Angeles all the way to San Francisco, crossing the Golden Gate bridge, as part of Amazon Heart Thunder USA 2008. And as we crossed that bridge many locals cheered us on, waving hands and shedding tears for loved ones they had lost.

Amazon Heart Thunder USA was a crazy, powerful and empowering experience for me. And it made me think very clearly that merely surviving cancer was not good enough, was not an option I could live with. The only way to go was to be, to Live; to dare and get out of my timid zone of fears and phobias…the list of which is too long to mention here.

But going back to my adventure with the Harley: I had no extra money for motorcycle lessons or the jacket, boots, helmet, gloves…and using funds from our already deflated budget (after surgeries I was too weak to resume a full-time job) was not an option. And then, just like that, amazing stuff kept happening. My motorcycle lessons at Farleigh Dickinson University were paid off by a sponsor, and my leather biker's gear was sponsored by the Bergen County (NJ) Harley-Davidson dealership, which also hosted a raffle fundraiser and helped me raise over $8,000 for the Amazon Heart organization. How awesome is that! And so I was able to join the Girls of the Amazon Hearts, twenty-four breast cancer survivors from the UK, Germany, Australia, Canada and the USA, for the Amazon Heart Thunder USA 2008 ride from Los Angeles to San Francisco.

I have a group photo of us in San Francisco, on the Golden Gate Bridge. And a photo of a lady with blue short hair, Blue, the most awesome person in our group, a software engineer, a biker and a good friend. She is the one who helped me obtain another photo of a gorgeous pretty lady who looks like a super model, with a humble smile and blue eyes. That is Alyssa Shiller, who passed away shortly after the event, never mentioning how ill she was during ten days of riding, smiling, sharing meals and a wine tasting in Pasadena…not a word; not a clue…always smiling and content with Life. Even on our last night at a San Francisco hotel, where I shared a room with Blue and Alyssa, she never mentioned being ill. An angel blessed her memory.

And that was the most outrageously awesome group of chicks riding their Harley-Davidsons, laughing at Mr. Grim, in an event orchestrated by an amazing couple from Australia who decided to share their love of Life with other Harley riders. The Girls with Amazon Hearts raised lots of funds to help the Amazon Heart organization support the Young Survival Coalition, a group focused on young women (some as young as eighteen!) who have been diagnosed with breast cancer.

I still have my cool leather Harley-Davidson jacket with diamonds and studs, my helmet with my biker name (Flame) painted on it by a local artist, my boots, gloves.... I cherish them all as trophies of my not-so-small victory of gaining my life back, not giving up easily and, along the way, sharing love, freedom and hope with others.

All that was also made possible by my amazing mother, who flew from Israel to stay with my family and help out with my children while I was gone. She has always been the real force behind all my achievements, as well as a source of courage and a true survivor who does it all with a beautiful smile and much charm.

Allysa Schiller
SF 2005
www.amazonheart2004-2010.org/AHThunder/default.htm

Lissa Williams, "Blue", Amazon Heart Thunder
Los Angeles, CA 2005

Part 4

My mother has lived in Israel for over forty years in the same two-bedroom apartment on the second floor of the long pink building with its views of the Mediterranean Sea and of a distant mosque above the valley. When my sister phoned about her trip to Odessa with our mother, I did not have the chance to tell her about my own planned journey to Odessa with Mom; but mine was a different kind of trip. Since moving to America I had gone to Israel to visit my mother almost every year, but this year I also had in mind to go back to Odessa with my mother. To be more precise, I wanted to visit Odessa via my mother's memories, which I would then write down and attach to my other letters to you.

This is what my mother told me on my last visit:

LETTER FIFTY-SIX: THE JEWELRY BOX

Every time I visit my mother, it seems her apartment remains almost untouched. It looks just as it did the day we buried my father: his paintings and swords...the African masks...the shelves with sculptures...the lacquered jewelry box, everything is always in the same place. The lacquered jewelry box remains in my mother's bedroom. Decorated with fuzzy flowers and dusted with gold, it is centered on a white dresser near the bed, close to her eyes and her heart. Pretty thing this box is. Designed in the French style of Vernis Martin, it was a gift my father gave to my mother on their seventeenth anniversary. The type of lacquer used on it was named after the French brothers Guillaume and Etienne-Simon Martin, and the style imitated the Chinese lacquer that was wildly popular in the court of Louis the XIV. Do you remember we saw a similar décor style while visiting the Louvre, in Marie Antoinette's bedroom? My father Emil used to say that this box is the same as the one of Marie Antoinette, but I thought he was just joking, lovingly comparing my mom to the queen.

Besides a few papers, my mother still stores her jewelry in her jewelry box, the last gift my father gave her.

LETTER FIFTY-SEVEN: A REQUEST

My mother greeted me as always with a warm smile and a table loaded with baked goods, but before we settled in her kitchen to talk we walked around her apartment. Following my look at one point to what was centered, as always, on her bedroom dresser, Mom lifted her lacquered jewelry box and said "Let's have a cup of coffee and cake..." Then she led the way to her sparkling kitchen where she had spread a white linen tablecloth over her mahogany table. I gladly followed, anticipating familiar flavors and her signature hospitality of fresh brewed coffee and chocolate cake.

In the kitchen with its familiar porcelain plates and shelves with silver pots, Mom gently placed her jewelry box on the table. After we had sipped fresh coffee and chatted about this and that and life in America, I finally asked my mother what had long been in the back of my mind: "Can you finish your story about Fergana?"

LETTER FIFTY-EIGHT: FERGANA

To my surprise my mother did not even blink, as if she had been waiting all these years for me to ask.

"Growing up," she said, continuing where she had left off during my last visit, "I barely knew my father Israel Davidovich Berdichevski, your grandpa Izya; I barely saw him at all. In 1939 when I was two, he was deployed to the battle of the Winter War. That is how people called the war between Russia and Finland; it lasted from November 30th, 1939 to March 13, 1940. But you know all that already, right?

"After returning from that war," my mother continued, "my father was decorated with many bravery medals and, as an important veteran, found a high-rank position within the Soviet Militia of Odessa processing passport applications. How to say Pasportnuy Stol; in Russian it means literally a table for passports, where they actually made those legal documents, sealing them with an ink stamp. People feared yet greatly respected my father as a powerful bureaucrat; and he always tried to help out and worked there until the beginning of Word War II.

"Your grandpa Izya was an educated man who had graduated from Odessa Tech, unlike my mother

Valya, who lost her father (my grandfather Alexander Schneider) in her early childhood and was forced to find a job to help out her family."

After a long pause, my mother added, "You know, that was never an issue for my mother, who turned into a very smart and strong woman and raised four children (Danya, Mery, Bebah and me) during a time of starvation in Odessa after the war. Raising one child then was hard enough, but four.... She did the impossible....

"The war was horrific, and even though I was only three years old, I still remember it all very well. Late on the summer evening of June 22, 1941, the sounds of a thunderstorm got mixed with heavy rain and loud strange noises coming down from the sky of Odessa; those were German airplanes buzzing above, covering the sky like they were black bats... and carrying bombs.... Your grandma Valya grabbed my little hand, pulling me as fast as she could, running alongside other people all around us. And each time a loud flash of lightning was followed by fire and smoke hitting the ground, she threw me down, covering my little body with her own heavy one; she was nine months' pregnant....

"I was lying down on the wet ground, barely daring to breathe, waiting for all the noise to go away. And once it quieted down, Grandma Valya rose above me and I could resume catching my breath, only to continue running all over again among other scared people. That was my first encounter with the war," my mother said, lowering her probably cold-by-now cup of coffee.

"Nu vot...you see...," she said, pouring freshly brewed coffee into my cup since I had already gulped all mine down, forgetting about the chocolate cake.

"Eat, I just made it," she said, placing in front of me a golden plate with a generous slice of cake. The chocolate smell teased my nostrils, but her story evoked a much larger appetite. Mom is a great story-teller, as her Aunt Ida was.

"Once the war began," she said, "the Germans started attacking Russian cities. You know the sto-ry of my grandmother Dora, who left Odessa, and how shortly after the German troops marched in and killed and raped and sent away so many people to concentration camps.

"At that point the city of Odessa summoned the evacuation of the remaining population, and your grandfather Izya was ordered by the army to a very responsible position: He was appointed to be the Commandant of Odessa responsible for Complete and Final Evacuation of Odessa's civilians. You see?" my mom said, as if I had not heard this story many, many times.

"He was assigned to a large ship named Lenin, the last passenger ship waiting in the port of Odessa for all the civilians, and it would wait until the last one had boarded. No one was to be left behind, he was told. His job was to organize all the people, not just the willing ones, but also the many that had re-sisted abandoning their beloved Odessa and wished to stay and fight the German enemy.

"Grandpa Izya went to each house, knocking on doors one by one, and assisted with packing as well as convincing, and forcing, residents to leave their homes, assuring them that in the near future he would bring them back home, free of the enemy, the Germans…. Many people refused and he had to drag them away from their homes, stores, gardens, family cemeteries….

"Me, my mother, her sister Sofia, Grandma Malka, and Aunt Ida Lopatinski (from Brighton Beach, yes,) who was married to my mom's brother, and all the neighbors, plus acquaintances as well as complete strangers… Grandpa Izya forced them all out and transported them all to the port to board the ship.

"Grandpa Izya refused to board until the last minute. When the ship finally blew out its last smoke announcing its pending departure from Odessa's port, he was still waiting on the pier, questioning if only one person had been left behind. He was finally lifted on the ropes as the departing ship left Odessa's port," my mother said, her eyes locked on a distant past….

"The conditions on the ship were terrible: There was no air, with many packed people taking turns to sit or lie down to rest, all throwing up, crying, fearful of their unknown destiny of waiting in a new land… thinking of leaving behind their beloved Odessa….

"How is the cake?" my mother said; to my own

astonishment I found myself craving her story as much as I craved the cake. My mother brushed her hand against my palm to reclaim my gaze, but I was far from asleep; I was on that pier with my grandpa Izya, a young strong soldier, waiting for the last passenger, refusing to leave as the ship kept puffing its white smoke and blasting its siren, signaling departure.... Hurry, Grandpa...hurry up....

"And when the ship exhorted its final signal," my mom said, "...but I told you that already, right?"

I didn't reply as I enjoyed the cake generously covered with sweet scarlet cherries I always left on my plate; they reminded me of the taste of a cough syrup from my childhood. Digging out the cherries despite my mother's disapproving look, I kept tentatively listening.

"It all seems like it happened yesterday," she said.

"After the longest journey of my life, our ship finally arrived at the first available seaport, and from there all the passengers were transported to a train that would take us to our final destination...Near Asia, Uzbekistan, in the valley of Fergana.

"Grandpa Izya had received a Bronya, a delayed deployment to the Red Army, for one year, a great honor for his diligent service in the army during all the previous years serving his country. He was assigned a position at Fergana's army factory because Grandma Valya was on her last term and about to have a child, and I was only three years old. He was given a one-year delay to take care of his family, before deployment back to war."

LETTER FIFTY-NINE: THE PROMISE

"The train…going back to that…. There is something I must tell you; it is a terrible secret I carry all my life…. "

My mother explained that the train did not have closed passenger cars but open wagons in which the refugees were packed. She remembers it somehow started to snow and people covered her with a blanket. My mother also explained that, as a decorated war hero, Grandpa Izya had been placed in a wagon also occupied by a few doctors who could attend to his pregnant wife, Grandma Valya.

Tragically, the train wagons were filthy, the doctors shortly diagnosed my mother with chicken pox and Grandma Valya came down with Goraczkaa Reumatyczna, rheumatic fever, a terrible sickness that can affect the heart, the joints, even the brain. She was suffering terribly, and was told by the doctors there was no way she could breastfeed her baby with infected milk.

How could a baby possibly survive such conditions? As far as Grandpa Izya could see, there was no way a baby could survive and there was no way he—Grandpa Izya—could do anything to make sure a baby survived with so many others depending on him. In addition to his gravely ill wife and sick little girl, a literal train full of his family and hundreds of evacuees depended on him as they headed into an uncertain future in a distant land during a terrible war.

"The conductor kept announcing unfamiliar names each time our train stopped," my mother said, "Derbent, Tashkent…. And after a few stops, Grandma Valya went into labor and a perfect baby boy was born, the son Grandpa Izya had dreamed of. But then, right there, he had to make a horrible and unspeakable decision no father should ever face; the one we never talk about, the one he would mourn for the rest of his life…."

My mother excused herself, leaving the room; I could hear her soft sobs and gasps for air. When she returned to the kitchen she said, "The boy was a pretty pink color, chubby and healthy. Your grandpa Izya had no choice but to do what he did next. He ordered the doctors not to cut the umbilical cord. No one heard the baby cry, not even once.

"And then Grandpa Izya did the unthinkable," my mother continued. "He shouted out a few orders in the authoritative voice of a warrior to stop the train at once. And just like that, people listened to his orders. He paid the train conductor 130 rubles, all the money he had left, and then wrapped his baby son in a sheet, grabbed my little hand, holding in the other a large shovel. He shouted again for the conductor to wait for us…"—my mom reached out for something, but just waved both her hands in a circular motion—"…and we both walked away from the train.

"I was so scared but did not dare ask where we were going. After a short walk Grandpa Izya and I reached a small hill with lovely wildflowers. Oh, that's it, I thought, this must be a nice surprise to bring wildflowers back to my mommy and the stinky train…. But to my surprise, after climbing to the top of the hill, instead of collecting lovely flowers my father Izya started digging in the ground. Was he looking for potatoes, carrots or a treasure for the family he always took care of? Many silly thoughts went through my mind, pushing away the inevitable.

"My strong father was digging and digging, but there was nothing there besides the small empty hole in the ground, where he gently placed the baby after a tender kiss. He then cried out a few words and, thrusting the shovel into the ground, promised me right there that one day, after the war was over, we would return to this grave and bring the baby back home to Odessa for a proper funeral.

"Walking back to our train without exchanging a word seemed the longest way…."

LETTER SIXTY: IZYA AND THE WALKING DEAD

After the train arrived in East Uzbekistan carrying Odessa evacuees including my mother Alla and her family, my grandfather Izya was assigned an important post at the armament factory of the Fergana Valley.

The valley was a picturesque place; it straddles Uzbekistan, Kyrgyzstan and Tajikistan east and is divided by five regions: Fergana, Andijan, Namangan, Khujand in Tajikistan and Osh in Kyrgyzstan. My mom's family was in the East Uzbekistan region of Fergana, near the city of Andijan, in the crossroads of two major rivers: Syr Darya and Kara Darya. My mother kept describing the place where they lived in the Fergana Valley as a desert of sand with long white buildings and an Arik across it, in the middle of nowhere; Arik, as the locals called it, is a river in Uzbekistan.

Desert and river, you say? How could that be! But that is how it was, as my mother recalls. She showed me an old photo of the river with the long building with a stable and a horse on the first floor, and desert all around. The house was in the middle of nowhere, just as she described it. How could my mother recall it so well? After all, she was merely three years old at the time!

The building had one large room assigned for the entire Berdichevski clan: Grandpa Izya, Grandma Valya, who was sick after labor, her little toddler with chickenpox (my mom Alla), Great-Grandma Malkar (Valya's elder mother), Aunt Sofia, Ida with her family…. Many people to fit in one room, but everyone was very happy to have a dwelling in this new land. Better something than nothing, everyone said gratefully.

On the other side of the building was a large stable, warmer than the room, with light and windows and a carriage with a beautiful horse.

Next day the curious local folks arrived to see who were the important people the army allowed to reside in this huge building and also gave a horse and a carriage! Meanwhile, all the children of the family were on a mission to sneak inside the stable and snatch Makucha, green leftover disks from cold-pressed sunflower seeds, from the horse. Apparently the horse was fed very well, better than the children, as he was the only lifeline for the family: Because of the horse Grandpa Izya could go to work, to the market in town or for a doctor far away in the city.

"Look at this photo," my mother said. "I had such tiny hands and such a skinny body. My job was the most important one: My cousin would lift me up in the air towards the Fortachka, a window leaf, and as I climbed into that small opening, I would take tightly pressed circles of Makucha, flat scones of leftovers from cold-pressed sunflower seeds after the oil was extracted. At three, I was a typical child of the war, the title my generation was called. Like you have something in America: Generation X, Y, Millennials…," my mother said.

"We were children of the war generation," she repeated, "and luckily the frozen irrigation ditch we called River Arik saved us from starvation, because all the hungry children would run there to scrape frozen shavings with our little hands, place those shavings into old iron Kazan pots, melt it for fresh water and mix that with the green Makucha."

The taste of the Arik water mixed with Maku-cha in a murky green soup was on my lips by now, mixed with chocolate cake. And each day spent in Fergana became my own, as real as the kitchen I was sitting in now, with my mother, in the pink building of Afridar.

I could see Grandpa Izya returning from a day working at the factory, riding in the horse carriage, arriving by the door of the building in the middle of nowhere in Fergana Valley. Young and pretty Grandma Valya and her skinny three-year-old daughter, my mom, ran cheerfully out to greet him while he reached into his pocket and retrieved an old cup of steamy Voyenuy Payok, a daily meal assigned by the army for each soldier. But Grandpa Izya saved his modest meal for his little girl and sick wife. He reached inside his Gimnasterka, uniform, once more, a smile spreading over his tired face. This time his empty hand appeared as if by magic with a cup of Kasha, porridge, followed by a slice of black sourdough bread. Finally, Grandpa Izya would conjure not one but two logs of wood to warm up the freezing room with its Chugunka, a cast iron stove with a pipe that went through the ceiling and a sideways small door for the logs. And atop the stove, as always, sat a large kettle of boiling water from the Arik.

Although the family apartment was just one long and large room with a few windows and a few plain beds, the poor conditions never interfered with the kindness and warm hospitality of Grandpa Izya and Grandma Valya. Grandpa became renowned for spending his spare time from his job at the factory riding his horse and carriage to visit the local market with only one purpose in mind: to pick up the Walking Dead, the living skeletons. That was the name given by locals to newly arrived people from Odessa, many of whom Grandma Izya knew as formerly rich, but who by now had turned into skinny starving skeletons. Every time Grandpa Izya went to the bazaar he would look for them and bring them over to eat something and get warm by the stove, away from that freezing desert.

"Among the many skinny people," my mother said, "were professors and shoemakers who once were very wealthy prior the war, but now were ill and incapable of adjusting to the cruel conditions of wartime: the hunger, the freezing desert weather, the poverty and lice. Your grandpa Izya would cover their shivering bodies on the floor of our living room in Fergana, gather them closely to the Chugunka and feed them with a teaspoon of sweet warm tea, as this was the only food we had. And your grandma Valya would take care of those sick people until they were able to take care of themselves; and that became a regular circle of our dwelling. Once the ill got better, they left to look for work as Grandpa Izya kept bringing new sick people in need of food and warmth. And that is how we lived," concluded my mom, as though stating a simple matter of fact.

How I wish I had known all that before, when Grandpa Izya was still alive. Maybe I would have paid more attention and had more patience and a better understanding of my grandfather's bitterness and depression in his old age.

After immigrating to Israel in the late '70s, Grandpa Izya and Grandma Valya lived in a small apartment in Sderot, the southern town where my family first lived in Israel. Grandpa Izya mostly liked to sit on a small chair by the window, on the second floor of their building.

Each time I visited Grandma Valya and Grandpa Izya in Sderot, all I saw was an old cranky man who barely ever smiled, taking care of plants gathered in small pots on the small table by the kitchen window. My mother once said that he had brought all those plants from Odessa; one from his mother Dora's grave, one from his son Danya's grave and another from the grave of Yuzic.

But I remember my Grandpa Izya as a very a bitter man who wore old sweatpants, Valenki, felt boots, and Kaftan, a sleeveless jacket made of sheep leather. He gave me both to keep me warm later on. You see how his generosity never ceased? He always shared the little he had left. As when your daddy and I got married in Israel and moved into a studio by the beach, Grandpa Izya gave us his old white refrigerator he had received from the Sohnut, the absorption department for new immigrants. But I was too silly to see the man behind the shadow of old Grandpa Izya sitting in the kitchen by his plants, probably thinking about all that had happened, and how he was now just an old man, stripped of all his heroic war days, losing his son, and one other.... All I could see was just an old cranky man. You see how silly I was? I had no patience at all, just like you nowadays, no patience for my stories. And that is why I wrote you my letters, in the hope that you will read them one day.

Sitting at my mother's kitchen table, staring at the last cake crumbs on my plate, I thought of my mother as a little skinny starving girl in the frozen desert of Fergana, stealing sunflower pancakes from a horse....

LETTER SIXTY-ONE: MISSING IN ACTION

Shoving away my plate with its cake crumbs, I said: "So what about your Grandma Dora, the one who left Odessa to go to Siberia before the Germans marched in, before your family evacuated to Fergana? What happened to her during the war?"

"Ah...," Mom said, "my lovely grandma Dora Izrailevna Berdechevskaya was a clever lady who left for Siberia before authorities ordered the evacuation of Odessa. This is what happed to her: Your grandpa Izya with his high-rank status of a war hero was able to locate my grandmother Dora (his mother) all the way in Siberia, where she had established herself as a very popular and prosperous tailor. Look at this photo of Grandma Dora, who always dressed up so elegantly, and me standing by her side with a pretty dress she made out of nothing.

"Grandpa Izya wrote a letter to his mother Dora in Siberia, explaining that he was being deployed again, and asking her to come to Fergana and stay to help care for my mother, me and my sister, who was born earlier that year. One sunny day the door of our room opened wide. First I saw a huge brown Sunduk, a leather trunk, followed by my grandma Dora, who had arrived all the way from Siberia! That is the kind of a woman she was, a clever, strong, warm and loving lady. Many stories and tears of joy were shared that day along cups of hot tea, as Grandma Dora told us how she survived in Siberia. She had many funny stories, like the one about the folks who were looking for her horns, since they had never seen a Jew," my mom concluded.

Hm...seems not much has changed since 1941. Recently I met a woman who exclaimed I was the first Jew she'd ever met, and added that I didn't really look anything like a Jew. I cannot even repeat all the B-S she said about what she had learned about Jews in her Sunday School classes, but each time I see her I pretend not to recognize her. We are in the twenty-first century, living in America, not in isolated Siberia of 1941.

"Everyone loved my grandmother Dora back in Siberia," my mother said. "She was a hardworking lady, smart, educated, a wonderful housekeeper, very neat, an amazing cook and a skillful baker. And years later, when I met your daddy Emil, she invited us to stay with her for the first eight years of our marriage! In one little cooperative room, Dora, me, your daddy, your sister Magusha and you, until you turned six and the government finally gave us a separate dwelling. All those years I tried to learn from my grandmother Dora as much as I could, and I will be forever grateful for all her teachings.

"But going back to Fergana: My father Izya was deployed to war again, and Grandma Dora arrived from Siberia to help raise his small family. My mother Valya slowly regained her strength under the loving care of Grandma Dora, and was able to work a few hours at the local bakery, getting paid with a daily loaf of bread instead of money. Carrying that loaf of bread on her way to our small apartment, my mother would pass by the markets and exchange a few slices of bread with local vendors for butter or a few eggs here and there, which she would then bring home with the rest of the bread. Smart, clever lady was my mother Valya, Zemplya ee Puxom, the ground will be her soft down.

"Meanwhile, Grandma Dora used to color strips of Marlya, gauze, and sew those thin strips into a large cloth, turning it into dresses and skirts for my little sister Mery and me. See what a clever lady she was? At that time I was assigned a few responsibilities too. At the age of five, my job was to care for my sister Mery and also do some errands, mainly at the grocery by our small apartment in Andijan, where we lived by now, thanks to Grandma Dora's savings from Siberia. We were also receiving a small military pension for my father Izya's deployment in Germany.

"Besides a few errands and watching my sister, I also had a real paid job: The year was 1943, and many soldiers were returning home injured, missing an eye, with no legs or one arm. Jobs were created and that's how I got my first job when I turned five. I had to stand by a blind soldier who played a harmonica and sing sad war songs I still recall: 'The Dark Night,' 'The Path,' 'The Fire Playing in the Wood-burning Stove'.... I still remember those melodies and words I sang along with the blind soldier as I watched to make sure passersby threw coins in his hat, not just little rocks that sounded like coins. After I spent a long working day singing with the soldier, he paid me with half a loaf of bread, and I ran back home so proud and happy to share it with my family.

"But one day my mother Valya came home crying, telling us about the letter she had received announcing my father Izya was missing in action near Berlin in Germany. And from that day on, even my half loaf of bread did not make my mommy smile, although we kept receiving military assistance of a small pension to help us survive. Nu, see how vse Zakonomerno (things are naturally supposed to happen)? See for yourself, as what happened next was against all odds, and Destiny had another plan for my father Izya.

"During the war, my father was assigned to drive an amphibian car, but later on he was promoted to become a private chauffeur for an important general, I forget his name. One day, the general summoned my father Izya to drive him to the forest near Berlin, a well known place with heavy German artillery and bombers from above. Driving through the forest they were caught in the middle of heavy artillery and had to find shelter. My father Izya dug a small hole the size of an animal burrow by a large oak tree to find refuge from the bombs. You know what happened next? His general ordered him out of his refuge, and my father, poor soldier, had no choice but to obey the general. He ran away, searching for another shelter, as the general comfortably crawled inside the burrow.

"While the fire balls from hissing bombs exploded all around, turning huge forest trees upside down and exploding aged roots, my father Izya managed to find a small hole. And after it all quieted down, he ran back to his car to resume driving the general to the Headquarters of Command, but to his astonishment his general was nowhere to be found! He ran back to the place where he had left the general and saw a huge hole in the ground at the bottom of the burrow with leftover body parts spread around mixed with dirt and tree roots. Nu vot, smotri (See?)…Zakonomerno…."

LETTER SIXTY-TWO: VICTORY DAY

"And now I return to telling you about the period of our life when we lived in Andizan not far from Fergana. We had moved into a small two-room apartment during the war, by a grocery store, thanks to Grandma Dora's savings earned in Siberia. Shortly after we moved in, Grandma Dora fell ill with terrible malaria. People all around were dying of things like malaria and starvation.

And as I told you before, my mother Valya worked and so did I, singing and caring for crippled soldiers. And that is how time passed by. Grandma Dora got better, my mother kept receiving a small pension for my soldier father who was missing in action, and life went on until…"—my mom paused to breathe and make sure she had my full attention—"…one day we all woke up from a terrible noise, and ran in horror outside our home, into the street near the market, to see what had happened. And then we saw what it was all about: All around the market street, as far as we could see, was an ocean of people with wide-open eyes, not scared but acting strange: singing out and clapping hands, hugging each other, crying, kissing, yelling…chaos, but I was not scared because it was a happy chaos, unlike the one we had experienced when my mother threw me on the ground back in Odessa, shielding me with her heavy body, pregnant with my baby brother that we had to bury on the hill.…

"I ran as fast as I could to the grocery in our building, where all the soldiers got together, where I would sing with a blind soldier, and they told me what had happened: Hitler was Kaput, gone, done with. That day was May 9, 1945. World War II was over.

"My mother Valya and Grandmother Dora were terrified, to my amazement, instead of filled with joy and ecstasy as people all around us were. They had no idea what they would do next, now that the war was over. I remember my mother writing many

letters to Odessa, trying to find out if some of our
friends or relatives had survived the war. And after
many letters, one day we received a letter that said
Aunt Sofia and her husband, Grandma Manya and
Aunt Ida with her three little children (Alexander,
living now in New York City; Pavel, living now in
Sydney, Australia; and Dorochka, Zal") were all living together in Odessa, and wanted us to join them!
'God help us all,'" the letter concluded.

"We immediately packed as fast as we could and
got on a train back to Odessa to join our surviving
relatives. And once arriving in Odessa, my mother
Valya, grandmother Dora, little sister Mery, and I all
joined our remaining family: Aunt Sofia, Grandma
Manya, Aunt Ida (from Brighton Beach) and her
children…all the people living in one room.

"V testnote da ne v obidu," my mother finally
said, which translates to something like "Cramped
yet not insulted."

"After a while," my mother added, "my family decided to see what had happened to our home
we lived in before the war in the Krasnuy Pereulok,
house number 28, apartment 23, Odessa."

LETTER SIXTY-THREE: KRASNUY PEREULOK

"My mother Valya went to see what had happened to their home, but when she returned, she was
so sad. Dvornichka, a floor sweeper maintenance
person known as Dunya, now lived in our pre-war
apartment. A plump, mean and bitter woman, she

refused to talk to my mother or even let her stand on the threshold of the house. Just like that, we were not allowed back in our home, and were forced to look for a small apartment nearby.

"Time went by and we lived as well as we could under harsh circumstances after the war."

LETTER SIXTY-FOUR: IZYA'S RETURN

"It was in the beginning of 1946 when we were all woken up by a loud banging on our door followed by a wide-opened door and a soldier standing on the threshold. He was young, very handsome, beaming with health, his broad shoulders heavily decorated with hanging medals and Red-Star orders. That was my father Izya! Yes, after all the years of Missing in Action during the War in Germany....

"After we all shared tears of joy and initial shock, he explained what had happened to him during the years he was missing. In the 1944 battles of Berlin, there where heavy fights with the Nazis and he was badly injured in one of them. He ended up with his ribs and both legs broken. As my father Izya lay in the battlefield all broken and unconscious, his fellow soldiers thought he was dead; they returned after the battle looking for his body to bring home for a proper funeral. But they could not find him anywhere, and that is how he was declared as Missing in Action, and we received a letter in Andijan informing us of this.

"But you want to know what really happened to

him? Well, after that battle, a kind German lady who lived in a nearby village found his broken body in the battlefield and took him to her village, where she cared for him until he got well and could walk again.

"I wish to find that lady and thank her for saving my father. I remember as clear as though it was yesterday how happy I was to have my father back, and to no longer be a poor orphan."

LETTER SIXTY-FIVE: HOMECOMING

"The day of my father's return, he learned about our house being occupied by fat and mean Dunya, the groundskeeper, and at once ordered us all to come along with him. I will never forget the scared expression on Dunya's fat grizzled face when she saw us all. Apparently my father Izya, the decorated soldier with medals and honor stars hanging on his broad shoulders, made the right impression; she swore to leave the apartment by dawn.

"The next morning, our little clan all arrived at the apartment with our belongings, but the house stood empty with bare walls, completely stripped of all that had been there. My father Izya then understood why Dunya needed one night to leave: She had completely emptied our house. Oh well, God will forgive her. We were so happy to be together again in Krasnuy Pereulok, the home of our family for over seventy years."

My mother got up to bring us another tray of baked goods, which smelled so good.

"And this is how my father divided the house for everyone," my mom continued, "Aunt Sofia and her husband received a room with a door leading outside; Grandma Manya was placed in the hall that connected all rooms with the small kitchen so she would always be warm. My father, mother, Mery and I got two tiny rooms. And the large kitchen served us all as a place to warm up; it was my family's favorite gathering place. While others cooked and fried foods, my father Izya chopped white cabbages in preparation for sauerkraut with red currants that would be kept in the wooden barrels beneath the kitchen. He also made pickles out of green cucumbers, green tomatoes, apples and watermelons, as the women cooked jam from leftover fruits for harsh winter days. Our apartment was always stocked with barrels filled with pickled food for family and many guests."

LETTER SIXTY-SIX: LIVING ARRANGEMENTS

"My father Izya, a decorated war hero, returning after years of being declared missing, was able to get back our house, but he also was able to get back the cottage his mother Dora had lived in with her family before the war. It was the same little cottage both her sisters lived in with their children, their ill father and pretty Genya. All perished in Auschwitz, besides pretty Genya, who was raped by German soldiers, and hanged.

"And that same cottage was the house your daddy Emil and I lived in after we got married. Grandma Dora invited us to live with her, in that small apartment on the second floor of her family cottage in Kirov Street, number 114. You see this photo of Grandma Dora sitting in a chair and Daddy and I, twenty-one and twenty, standing near? I was very happy in that photo, looking forward to sharing my life with this handsome young man who played violin and piano and was so smart and funny.

"We lived with Grandma Dora in one small communal room, sharing one large kitchen and bathroom with other tenants. We lived there until 1966 when Grandma Dora passed away.

"The conditions were harsh and not always easy, yet somehow all the tenants tried their best to live in mutual coexistence and respect. The word privacy was not in our vocabulary. One woman, a piano teacher, respectfully dumped her diabetic husband's frequent urine in the communal kitchen's large sink, as he was too embarrassed to do it himself. The wife always addressed her sick husband as Mister, never by his first name, and all the tenants out of respect looked the other way each time she walked into the kitchen carrying his green glass bottle," my mother said.

The memory is a strange thing. I can actually remember Great-grandma Dora at that cottage always having a Smorshenoye, a wrinkled apple, for me during cold winter days. She had a funny-looking table, carved in oak, with a secret drawer we all knew about. There she would store a few red apples from the summer. The wrinkled apples were sweet, scarlet red and well preserved despite the cruel Russian winters. It was my favorite dessert; besides Masha's Barbariska candies, of course.

"During that time," my mom continued, "I worked at the Construction Bureau, and being a parent to little children—you were two and your sister was four—I became eligible for the government waiting list for a lottery to get our own apartment. At the same time, our studio was working on a new development in Odessa, Cheromushki, and we were a very lucky family for this opportunity to have our own place, away from communal dwelling. After living with my Grandmother Dora for eight years, we finally moved into a new building apartment with two bedrooms on the second floor in Cheromushki, and lived there until June 1971...."

LETTER SIXTY-SEVEN: MANYA

"Did I tell you about my grandma Manya? She became very religious in her late years, strictly observing the Jewish laws of Kashrut and covering her hair, daily attending Synagogue. We all highly respected all that. And in the evening, upon returning from Synagogue, she was busy preparing fruit spread, and placing it in small glass jars. People came from all over our town to bring clothing for her to mend or just wash, and Grandma Manya would wash, sew, hem whatever was needed and, when giving things back, she always added a small jar of glass filled with

her fruit spread. She somehow knew what was needed. When visiting people she would also bring along
her small jars of jam.

"Grandma Manya was always busy as a bee
until the end of her life in February 1970, in her
bed, surrounded by children, grandchildren, many
great-grandchildren and all the people who loved
her. God bless her soul," my mother said.

It seems I got it from my mother, her way of
drifting in circles from subject to subject, yet somehow bringing it home, connecting it all at the end.
But of course she does it so much better than I and
I need to learn from her. Bringing it home, I mean.

LETTER SIXTY-EIGHT: SHOCKS AND SURPRISES

"Back in Odessa after the war, all seemed to get
back to normal. In 1952 my father Izya got a prestigious job as Zavsklad, quartermaster, at Odessa's
main storage quarters, a sure path to becoming powerful and well connected. Meanwhile, my mom Valya
assumed a position at a local deli. Thus it seemed the
worst was left behind and the future seemed bright
and promising, finally filling us with hope, until Destiny shocked us all again.

"The first shock happened in 1966 when my
grandma Dora went out for a daily visit to my father
Izya to bring him his favorite lunch, Vareniki Vareniki, dumplings with meat. But on her way there she
had a stroke.... She died shortly after, never gaining
back her consciousness. And my father Izya could

never get over it.

"The second shock came in 1970, when we lost my young brother David, Danya. My father was never himself again. He suddenly aged in one day, losing his black hair color to a dull gray, his posture turning him from a proud veteran into a bowed man with staring wide eyes with nothing to see beyond Toski I Pechali, sadness and sorrow. Nothing mattered to him now besides visiting the cemetery.

"Each morning at dawn, my father Izya shuffled his feet as he carried a bucket, a rag and a fresh bunch of flowers to the cemetery where he stayed until late evening, caring for the graves of his mother Dora, his son David (Danya) and later for Yuzic (Josef), my baby sister Bebah's husband. Seems life had stopped for my father...."

After pausing, my mother said, "You know, your daddy Emil was the only one my father Izya still listened to, and so he listened to Emil's advice to leave Odessa, to start anew and join us in Israel (We arrived in June '71, remember?); there was nothing left in Odessa besides that cemetery, your daddy Emil kept writing him.

"But it took a few years until 1975 when my mother Valya, father Izya and both my sisters with their families were finally allowed to leave Odessa and immigrate to Israel. They all lived in the small town of Sderot, in the south near the Gaza Strip, the same town where we lived in the Sohnut absorption center for our first six months in Israel. But it was

too late for them to see your father Emil. He was
gone by then."

Alla (left), Dora (middle) and Izya
with little Danya (left) with young
Bebbah on the upper row
Odessa 1953

LETTER SIXTY-NINE: IZYA AND VALYA

"My father Izya was completely ruined after
your daddy Emil died. He was devastated and from
then on all he cared about was the cemetery back
in Odessa. Who would take care of the graves of
Dora, Danya, Yuzic...? He also greatly suffered for
not knowing the Hebrew language and being unable
to communicate with locals. Shortly after his arrival
in Israel, my father Izya suffered from a stroke, but
unlike his mother Dora, he did not die. Being much

younger, my father Izya got away with partial paralysis that was followed by many other illnesses of a weak heart: high blood pressure, diabetes…..

"While my mother Valya was two years older, she was healthier than my father Izya and much stronger in her body and mind. She was a very realistic lady who took care of my father until 1988, when he fell ill and died at the same hospital by the Mediterranean Sea of Ashkelon where your daddy Emil died," my mom said.

I recall that my Grandma Valya was always a strong and independent lady who gave to others rather than take from them. I especially recall my visits to her Sderot apartment, where boxes under her kitchen table were filled with onions and potatoes. And whenever I left her apartment, I would discover a bag filled with potatoes and onions in my stuff; she always managed to sneak in some package filled with food, and whatever I brought over left back with me, in addition to her many packages and bags.

"Take, take, I don't eat so much, why I need so much…take it home," she used to say. She had a big heart and used few words.

Grandma Valya managed to give her warm smiles and baked goods to all until 1993; she was eighty years old when she had a stroke.

My mom Alla (known to all in Israel as Aliyah) worked at the Medical Center in Ashkelon, and my sister Margalit came over too, and both of them never left Grandma Valya alone. They fed her, washed her, massaged her with favorite creams and lotions, but nothing seemed to help; she lived for only one week at that hospital, dying in her sleep with a smile on her face, surrounded by children and grandchildren…. That happened on Friday, August 6, 1993. Mir praxu ee, bless her soul.

"We buried my mother Valya in Sderot," my mom said, "near my father Izya, to whom she was married for over fifty years, not always through easy times, but always with mutual love."

LETTER SEVENTY: EMIL AND ALLA

"How I met your daddy Emil? Ah, it all happened a long time ago in Odessa of the '50s. After graduating high school," my mom said, "I had to brush up on my math and physics for college, and after a thorough search we found Professor Usherovich. During one school session I met a young man who would change the course of my entire life. You see, Usherovich was teaching these same subjects to Emil Skulski, yes, your daddy Emil, and they both shared a passion and enthusiasm for chess, math and music.

"I remember once visiting my teacher, casually as in many previous times, arriving for my lessons in physics even before the door opened, and I heard a song, one I'd never heard before: It was 'Ave Maria.'"

And that is how my parents met: My mother Alla was sitting in the waiting room of her teacher and

couldn't move, she was so absorbed in those un-
earthly sounds she had never heard at her parents'
house, and when the last strains of the beautiful music quieted down, she walked into a large study room
and saw her teacher seated by the chess math table
in front of a young man with wavy hair. The men
did not notice her until after their game was over,
when her teacher introduced the young man as Emil
Skulski, Emka, his student. Mom introduced herself:
Alla Berdechevskaya, Alka.

"During that winter session we got to know each
other, talking, listening to music and learning physics. I learned that Emil came from a highly educated
family. His father worked as the head of math and
physics faculty at Odessa Institute; his mother had
graduated with honors from a high school for young
ladies in Odessa, as the only Jewish girl and the only
one who received a gold medal. His sister, Miya, had
graduated from the Mechnikov Odessa National
University, played fortepiano, and worked as a biology teacher at the evening school; his aunt, Dr. Maria
Tih, Masha, spent all of World War II until the fall
of Berlin working as a doctor to Russian soldiers.

"And Emil learned about my parents being good,
simple, hardworking people. Being from such different backgrounds, neither of us ever considered any
possible relationship...we were just friends. Meanwhile, your daddy graduated with honors from The
Odessa National Academy of Music, majoring in
playing the violin under the teachings of Olga Borisovna, that famous violinist. Emil graduated with

honors and played a concert that included Bach's 'Aria for Bass'…. Music and books were his entire world….

"Your daddy Emil introduced me to this unfamiliar world of music and books I was not even aware existed. We frequently went to the philharmonic and the opera, and I am forever grateful to him for opening a door to that magical world!

"Oh, I can see it's getting too long for you," my mother sighed. She was right: I was drifting away from the kitchen and soon the entire apartment had vanished, replaced with the city of Kishinev and my father Emil as a young man, vibrant and handsome, wearing a Sombrero, a colorful poncho casually covering his shoulders. I have a photo of him like this taken during the filming of Zapasnoy Igrok, a short comedy of the 1950s that became an international success. And though my mother was not in this photo, she was always by his side.

"Let me make my long story short for you," my mother finally said. "Emil was going to the city of Kishinev to work on a film. My Grandma Dora had once told me about a relative of her late husband who lived in Kishinev, however she didn't have his last name or current address. The only thing she knew about him was that before the war he worked as a very popular shoemaker in the central Street of Kishinev, the Lenin Street. When I mentioned to Emil my wish to travel to Kisheniv, I made an oath to look for this relative. All I knew was that his name was Gregory, or Grisha. As for your daddy Emil, apparently in that same town of Kishinev lived a family with very close ties to his. Both families had been evacuated to Uzbekistan during the war.

"So just like that we both had ties to Kishinev. Some people will dismiss this as coincidence, but I say there is no such thing. It's all the way it should have happened, and that was my destiny no one could change.

"You can't imagine our endless joy; we both were ecstatic as children when my family finally granted me permission to go to Kishinev. I took one week off my job and joined the troop of Odessa's filming studio. That one week changed the course of my life."

LETTER SEVENTY-ONE: WEDDING DAY

"Upon our arrival in Kishinev, Emil contacted friends of his family who welcomed us to stay over for that entire vacation. Those were very happy times! During the day Emil worked at the filming studio and in the evening we took long walks throughout the town. We had a wonderful time all that week basking in loving hospitality.

"On May 16, 1958, the filming studio was off, and Daddy and I took advantage of that and set off to explore the streets of Kishinev.

"The weather was pleasant and we decided to go for a walk. We always enjoyed those walks on the cobbled streets of the town, streets that were crowded with vendors selling all kinds of snacks: Cemech-

ki, black sunflower seeds, pan-fried right there on
a kerosene; Rachki, tiny dry shrimp; Ponchiks, big
dumplings filled with meat, apple or green peas....
The smells were everywhere and the food was very
cheap, offered in a cone folded from a newspaper.
There were no brown bags as you have it now.

"We admired the architecture of surrounding
buildings, some in Art Nouveau, others in a New
Roman style. And sometimes we found ourselves
in a narrow street with old shabby homes standing
there as a painful reminder of the war.... Such a horrific price the Russian people paid for the victory....

"As we casually browsed through the town that
day, all of a sudden we were standing on the Street
of Stephan the Great, Number 1: the City Hall of
Kishinev. Emil opened the door and I just followed
him without saying a word, as was my way, never
questioning him. Inside he began asking a secretary
a few questions and I was listening in shock, because
we had never discussed the idea of getting married, plus I didn't have my passport. Then the secretary said that in order to get married, we needed
to provide our passports and a permanent resident
of Kishinev as a main witness. I called my mother
right away, asking for my passport and explaining the
reason.

"The next morning my mother Valya and Grandma Dora arrived with pale faces at Uncle Grisha's
apartment and begged him to be our witness at the
ceremony. Seems Uncle Grisha really liked us and
happily agreed to witness the creation of such a

young and loving family.

"The happiest day of my life was May 17, 1958 (Emil was twenty-one; I was twenty), when I became the wife of Emil Skulski. And right after, we returned to my Uncle Grisha's residence to face an unexpected mirage-like scene.

My Uncle Grisha lived in a Patio behind an iron gate with a Venetian-style fence and a central paved courtyard separating studios from the garden. And, once the Patio gate opened, we all were stunned and I will never forget one of the most colorful pictures of my life: Right from the gate, all along the courtyard, were tables decorated with pretty flowers and fruits. Each family residing in the Patio had been invited to celebrate our happiness and brought over whatever they had to fill up the tables with plates of food, snacks, flowers and drinks. A Patephone played in the background and children were dancing…. That was my amazing wedding day and the only wedding I ever had!"

LETTER SEVENTY-TWO: THE COTTAGE

"After the wedding we went back to Odessa and my grandmother Dora invited us to stay over. We gladly moved in after freshly painting her cottage apartment, making a few adjustments for newlyweds. And you know the rest: We stayed with Grandma Dora for eight happy years, until getting the apartment in Cheromushki, were we lived until going to Israel."

My mother was looking through me, not realizing she had repeated the same story all over again. At the same time I was thinking about that cottage in Odessa, Kirov Street number 116, the same place in which Dora's extended family ceased to exist after Germans marched in, and her pretty niece Genya suffered her terrible destiny.... Luckily, my mother's voice rescued me from such dreadful thoughts.

"Nu," she said, "how about another cup of coffee?"

"Thanks," I said, relieved and glad for a few free moments to digest her stories, yet anticipating more to come.

Newly wed Alla and Emil Skulski with Dora
Odessa 1958

LETTER SEVENTY-THREE: EMIL

As I sipped from my cup of coffee, my mom said, "Now I will tell you my worst memory ever, because it's not even a real memory but my daily sorrow. Almost forty years have passed since your daddy Emil died, but I keep living my life as if he is right here, by my side. No hour goes by without me thinking about him, talking to him, telling all about his beautiful daughters growing up into good mothers, and his grandchildren and all he has missed since he is gone....

"You know why? Besides, of course, the sweet love we shared, it is because Emil was not an ordinary person: He was one of a kind, and because of that after he left this world, he also left behind unforgettable traces of character and thoughts in all the people who were lucky to know him.

"Your daddy Emil was loved by all, always in the middle of attention. He was a handsome, smart, intelligent, resourceful, kind man.... Obviously he also had a few flaws as any normal person, but his generosity and loving personality completely dismissed and compensated for them all. It was very difficult, almost impossible, to get mad at him. That is the reason I consider myself to be very lucky in life: I received a great gift—life gave me the present of meeting your daddy and spending seventeen unforgettable years by his side.

"Life with him went so fast, as one splendid moment, but with immense intensity and density, as though he could know his life would be very short and he was always in a hurry to take it all in: to see, to taste, to hear and to feel it all. Daddy lived as a man on a mission; he was a skillful fisherman, an actor, producer assistant, a hunter, competitive chess player and musician playing violin and piano. He also wrote short stories and painted. A sculptor, philatelist, designer of Sobel mink Russian hats, a photographer—remember his darkroom with the stinky liquids and hanging strips of negatives? He claimed our small pantry in Cheromushki as his darkroom studio. Of course I agreed, glad to watch him so happy in that little studio.... You see this metal stick? It's from Daddy's studio; I still keep it. Daddy used it to cut the negatives and glue parts of them back together to edit family films....

"I was always amazed by how handy he was. He could take apart a TV, a watch, a complicated structure, to run electrical wires and set up phone lines—he never even learned all that! He just knew how to do it," my mother said, leaving the kitchen.

She returned shortly, holding an old teddy bear with brown glass eyes and a missing ear. It was covered with a fading patch of red. I remembered how my sister used to play doctor with this bear; surgeries were her favorite procedure.

"When your sister was born, Aunt Miya bought her this soft furry teddy bear," my mother said, "but she could not find a similar one for you. Then, on

one summer vacation while cruising the cities of
Crimeria, Emil saw a very similar teddy in a store
window and was about to get it for you, but the store
was locked. Daddy was so upset and stated he was
not going back the ship without this bear, and he
couldn't care less if the ship left without him. He got
very stubborn and there we were, soaking wet from
a downpour of rain late at night. The ship was about
to depart, and your daddy Emil kept banging on the
door, gesturing with his hands to open it…. Who
could resist his charm?!" my mother said, leaving the
kitchen once again, returning this time with a gray
fur bear with a pair of plastic black eyes, a fat torso,
big round ears and large round feet.

My children, do you remember these two bears
in Israel, when we visited Grandmother Alla in
Ashkelon?

"Of course no one could resist your father Emil's
charm," my mother continued, "and the store door
was opened by a smiling lady who removed the gray
bear from the shop window and handed it to your
father as if he were her best friend ever. We took our
shoes off, oblivious to the rain and, happy as young
kids, ran back to the pier of the Ivan Franko."

LETTER SEVENTY-FOUR: THE RESTAURANT

"Almost every summer we went away on the Ivan
Franko, a Soviet ocean cruise ship, staying in the lux-
ury suite named 'Luks,' and many times your daddy
invited my parents, Valya and Izya, to come along.

"During one of those cruises, we were advised to visit a fascinating restaurant on top of a mountain by the Black Lake. Hours of driving on dusty narrow roads had us climbing higher and higher, leading us to the most spectacular place we ever saw, rewarding us with breathtaking views. We were on top of a mountain, surrounded only by the sky above and the sea below. There was a small structure with a local band playing exotic melodies and a few tourists feasting on Shashlik kebabs.

"Walking in, we noted a very strange scene for a place like this: In a distant corner by a small table a little girl was crying with her frightened parents. Your daddy Emil didn't think twice and approached their table. He was told they also were tourists and their ship was leaving tomorrow in the morning, but they had been so taken by this place they kept ordering more and more dishes without realizing the bill kept piling higher and higher, and now the owner of the restaurant was calling the police.

"Your daddy calmed them down and went to talk to the owner. Just like that. After a few minutes we saw the smiling owner approach that frightened family to say that all was settled and they were free to leave. The young man approached your daddy, hugging him as an old friend, insisting on having our address in Odessa so he could repay the debt, but your daddy Emil just smiled, saying that money is nothing, today I have it, and tomorrow you will have it. And besides, Daddy said, Life is like in that joke that only mountains never meet, but people always do. The young man kept insisting until your daddy told him we were from Odessa and tomorrow our ship Ivan Franco was departing back home, and we returned to our table, forgetting about the incident.

"The next morning at six o'clock someone banged on our suite door and summoned your father to the upper deck. We all got very nervous and didn't know what to think. Your father quickly dressed and I followed shortly after. The deck was filled with people as I made my way to the center of it, constantly searching for your father in the crowd. And there he was, as usual, in the middle of a group of young people.

Alla's parents, Izaya and Vala, with
Alla (far left), on a cruise
Crimea–Sochi 1964

"Approaching them, I recognized the couple from the restaurant. Apparently they had come over to our ship to pay their debt and they brought with them all their friends who were eager to meet Emil Skulski from Odessa! They were in a group of young people also from Ukraine who were working together, and they had all collected money to return back to your daddy. He was very embarrassed by all that attention.... They picked him up, throwing him in the air like some kind of celebrity, praising him not for merely paying for their friends, but mainly for his act of kindness to complete strangers.

"You see what kind of man your daddy Emil was?" my mother said.

LETTER SEVENTY-FIVE: A TRACE OF SUN

"When we arrived in Israel in 1971," my mother said, "we were all alone, no family, no friends; it was not easy. Only after a long year were our friends from Odessa finally granted a visa and happily arrived in Israel. They were Lyona, Petya, Izya, Zhora...all had been young pupils Zeida was teaching. It was as a family reunion and your daddy took them all under his wings; he took full responsibility for them and every evening we invited our friends over for a nice dinner with the best drinks and food. Although we were still newcomers ourselves in a new country, Daddy took great pride in taking care of his beloved friends.

"Daddy also insisted that our friends have an open account at the local grocery, telling the red-hair owner Mot'le that all his 'brothers' had arrived in Israel and they would come and shop and would never pay; he was the one to pay for it all at the end of the month. And since that day, after he got his paycheck, your daddy went to the grocery to cover all those expenses. He helped with painting his friends' apartments, assembled their furniture, built shelves…whatever was needed for his 'brothers,' as they all were as real brothers from our Odessa days, and all was done with love, never expecting a return. That is how your daddy Emil was.

"I truly believe that people like your daddy Emil are as shining stars: Once they arrive, their presence is illuminating, it warms up their surroundings. And with their departure, they leave behind an unforgettable trace deeply inscribed in those who came in any contact with them. But people like your daddy Emil, star people, are getting quickly shut down, burning fast yet leaving behind a profound feeling…how to say…something intangible yet warm as Topluy Zaychik, a trace of a sun," my mother said.

LETTER SEVENTY-SIX: THE KAZAN

"After your daddy Emil and I got married we went on fishing trips quite often, bringing along Emil's little nephew Devik, and my little brother Danya. And when your sister and you were born we brought you two with us. Here is a photo of your daddy with your sister and you on his lap, and another of me standing by a little hut in a remote village, and one of us fishing, and eating by a campfire.

Emil Skulski, fishing trip, 1960

"Each morning I went to the local market to trade freshly caught fish for local produce and fresh dairy products. Look at this photo of your daddy holding a huge fish that sustained us all for many days…. We used to cook a fish soup with a few potatoes, onions and carrots on a campfire inside a big Kazan, a cast iron pot. I kept this Kazan many years and brought it with us to Israel in 1971. And when you got married, and were living in Afridar in that cute little beach house, I gave it to you, remember? You used to make French fries in it until one day you threw it away because it got all black. Silly girl. It was the best part. They don't make pots like that anymore. Nowadays, pots are made of a cheap thin blend of aluminum that makes food taste bad."

My mother concluded her story without looking at me, making me feel worse than ever for throwing out the old Kazan with all of its precious memories. She was right, though: How silly of me.

LETTER SEVENTY-SEVEN: ROOTS

You see how many amazing stories I have to tell you before all this is lost and gone? What choice do I have but to keep writing all I remember?

Do you remember an assignment from your elementary school called Root Report, when you were asked to interview your ancestors and file your report in a folder with all the family history and photos? "Mom," both you and your sister exclaimed, "really, all that happened, all that is true? All those stories sound like a Hollywood movie."

And you made me think as I was telling you about this and that, about all that had happened; there were so many amazing stories from our family's journey about things that had also affected many other people of that time, and all that was too important to not document and just let fade away. Each one of us has a story to tell, don't we?

LETTER SEVENTY-EIGHT: TURKISH COFFEE

After I turned forty, my mother began making more sense to me, and I started to realize that something must be going on with the structure of our life, almost like tossing a deck of playing cards in mid-air, then staring at the cards as they landed as though organized by an invisible hand. And many times the final pattern begins to make some sense as all the pieces are somehow connected by an invisible tapestry of glue. Some people call this force a creator, others Haruach..., but the name does not change the item itself, the force, the glue, the handling hand.

"How is the cake? A cup of Turkish coffee?" my mother asked, and to my surprise I craved for more of her coffee as much as I longed to hear more of her stories, and though my eyelids felt heavy and I was getting tired from digesting both the coffee and the stories, my curiosity took over.

My mother got out a small stainless steel pot to brew us Turkish coffee. Everyone in Israel calls such a pot Finjan, but the Turks call it Cevze, and in America it is mostly called Ibrik (from the Greek Briki). Finjan is actually a name for a small glazed cup to hold Turkish coffee....

Very soon a strong aroma of Turkish coffee was spreading by the kitchen window beneath which my father Emil used to whistle the opening bars of a Tchaikovsky piano concerto, announcing his arrival.

LETTER SEVENTY-NINE: PERFECT CONDITION

"Now I'll go back to Fergana," my mother firmly said as if in an argument, but I was just waiting for her Turkish coffee, staring at my plate with its untouched cake crumbs, drifting back to Fergana, thinking again about my mother as a little starving girl in that place, stealing sunflower pancakes from the horse.

"Going back to Fergana," continued my mother, "my father was able to locate my grandmother Dora all the way in Siberia, where she had established a reputation as a popular and prosperous tailor. Look at this photo of Grandma Dora dressed up elegantly, and of me standing by her side, with a pretty dress she made of nothing."

Seems my family has always been very good at making pretty things from nothing. Even now, my mother was all dressed up very elegantly in a neat outfit she'd worn for more than forty years! She just doesn't ruin things, I guess. How does she manage to keep it all so neat and in perfect condition for so long? Like all her dishes, linens, statues, everything all over her apartment on the second floor in the pink building in Ashkelon. It's all in perfect condition, almost as though time stopped in that apartment on April 16, 1975, the day my father died.

LETTER EIGHTY: ZAHAR

"Ah…I think I told you already about Fergana, didn't I?" my mother said, pouring hot boiling Turkish coffee into cups in front of us.

"Yes, yes, I forgot I did. Then now, I will tell you about my Uncle Zahar. There is never a good time to tell of bad things happening to loved ones, and this story I tell you now is about Zahar, my father Izya's younger brother.

"Zahar's life turned out to be nothing but misery, a destiny shared by many young Jewish men. It was known that many Jewish boys would never return home from the Russian army, and Zahar, as many others, was seeking a way out, following a path of desperation and the unthinkable. And Zahar, as many others, shot his right hand, claiming it happened as an accident in hopes that he would be declared unfit to serve in the army.

"That miserable decision turned his life into a chain of suffering. During the military trial, Zahar's case turned into a political circus of a Jew who had betrayed his country. Zahar, as were many other young Jews in similar situations, was declared a traitor and sentenced to twenty years in Siberia's worst camps for criminals and murderers, a horrible place called Porilska and Magadana. Zahar was only twenty years old!

"My Grandma Dora was never the same again. The only assistance she could give her baby son was a monthly letter with a small package. From his letters, Grandma learned about the horrors of Siberia's camps, the hard labor, the cold weather of fifty Celsius below zero, the walking skeletons, the starving people.

"Meanwhile, World War II began, and Stalin had an idea to replace lost-in in-battle soldiers with new battalions made up of young and 'healthy' prisoners.

The main purpose of those battalions was to create a living wall as a shelter for others. Those soldiers were to be ready to die by exploding themselves under German tanks, and they carried grenades and Molotov bottles. The ones that died became national heroes; the ones that survived were to return to their Siberia camps to finish serving their terms.

"Zahar did not die as a hero, but survived and had to return to Siberia and serve his sentence until he was released in 1958. That same year I married your daddy Emil, and we moved in with Grandma Dora, as I told you.

"And shortly after, one day at Grandma Dora's apartment there was a loud knock on a door, and there stood a strange man with gray hair, missing all his teeth, staring like a wounded animal. That was my Uncle Zahar. All the misery was there, projecting all that had happened to him! And as if that wasn't enough, he had to face the reality of other convicted people; he wasn't allowed to live in a large city.

"Alas, Odessa, a wonderful tourist destination, a metropolitan port city on the banks of the Black Sea, was exactly such a city, and Zahar wasn't allowed in. So while 'visiting' his own home, he eventually had to leave to find a job and a place to live in the small town of Ackerman, located in Belgorod-Dnestrov, where he lived all alone, followed at night by the nightmares of Siberia. He suffered from despair, dissatisfaction and disappointment in all, and found the only one companion he could have: a bottle.... He was kicked out from his job and his apartment, until one day his luck changed.

"Zahar met a wonderful lady, Liza Parkanskaya, who was very poor yet beautiful and understanding. They fell in love and decided to have a family. And, thanks to her determined patience, dedication and love, they were able to stay together. A son was born, Lev. He is currently married with children, working as an accordion teacher in that same place, which is now Moldavia.

"For years while Grandma Dora was alive, Zahar and his family always came to celebrate the holidays in her apartment. But Zahar didn't live long; he died of cancer after many months of suffering."

You see how many stories our family has? Before it is all lost and gone, what choice did I have but to keep writing it all down? So I collected bits from here and there, making sense as I translated articles, poems and letters from Hebrew and Russian, and I put them all in this book. For you.

CONCLUSION: THIS MELODY CANNOT BE STOPPED

After having a cup of Turkish coffee, I looked at the lacquered jewelry box my mother had placed on the table earlier, and opened the lid to stare at the familiar items inside that I knew so well: my father's platinum pin, my mother's brooch with emeralds and pearls, my father's platinum wedding ring. On the lower shelf there were the usual two papers: One was a yellowish page from a local newspaper announcing my father's death; the other was a letter to

my mother ending with the words: "OR ELSE…"
and demanding the immediate end of an investiga-
tion into the possible murder of my father Emil.
What choice did my mother have as a newly wid-
owed immigrant in troubled Israel with two teenage
daughters? I was fourteen, my sister sixteen….

But there was something else among those two
familiar papers that I had never seen before: a fresh
page from a local newspaper announcing the death
of a man who was killed in a car accident. And in the
middle of the article was a photo of the same face
of the person who took my father's life.

Goosebumps of repulsion crawled up my spine,
awakening skeletons from the past, threatening to
bury me alive…again. Paralyzed with panic, I felt
sweaty drops replaced with beads of sweet revenge
as I forced myself to look at the picture again. I saw
the small empty eyes in the ugly red face with its
meaty misshapen nose and broad chin. It was the
same ugly mask I had seen once before. Shortly after
we buried my father, my mother and I saw an arro-
gant and very ugly man embracing a fragile lady who
carried a small child. I could never forget the smirk
on his face when he saw us. My mother grabbed my
hand, squeezing it hard, like she had done in Vienna when we faced German soldiers and their guard
dogs. Then came words I also would never forget,
as my mother squeezed them out between her lips:
"That is the man who killed your father."

As I stared once again at this repulsive mask, overwhelmed by the joy of sweet revenge but nonetheless unable to get rid of my sorrow for the widow and her son, I reached into my pocket for the papers I wished to place in my mother's jewelry box alongside her own. Under my mother's probing gaze, I placed inside the box two letters: The first contained the lyrics of my father's favorite Israeli song, which goes like this: "Et hamangina hazot i-efshar lehafsik…muchrachim lehamshich lenagen…" and translates to: "This melody cannot be stopped…we must keep playing…." These same words my mother had inscribed on an open book placed on my father's tomb. I have a photo of the white marble tower and the copper letters that spell out Emil Skulski, while an open Book of Life carries the copper lines of the melody he so loved.

As my mother kept watching, I placed my second document in the box. It consisted of two pages: The first page lists the names of all the people I wrote about in my letters, which are now in this book; and the other page is a parchment note from Jerusalem stating that, for each name from this list, a tree has been planted in Jerusalem. Yes, yes, for each and every soul I've mentioned in this book, a tree has been planted. A tree for Zeida, Polya, Gusta, Masha, Ehudif, Karl, Emil (Emka), Izrail, Valya, Danya, Dora, Alexander, Genya, Zahar, Yuzic, Samuel, Eve, Tomas, Yitzhak, Petya, Izya, Ina….

And here, this is for you: Ha, yes, yes, I kept this note for you of course; it is the address of that place in Jerusalem where all the trees were planted, so you can go visit them some day.

Gallery
of
Our Family
Photos

Valaya (upper left), Alla (left) Mery
(right) and Bebbah (center)
Arkadia beach, Odessa 1948

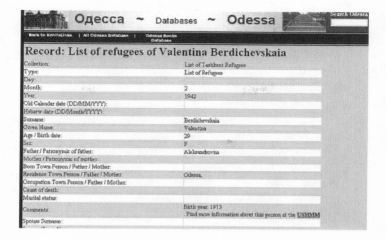

Odessa Refugee Card of Valya (Valentina
Alexandrovna Schneider{ Berdichevski})
Tashkent 1942

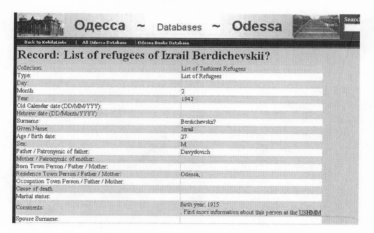

Odessa Refugee Card of Izya (Izrail
Davidovich Berditchevski)
Tashkent 1942

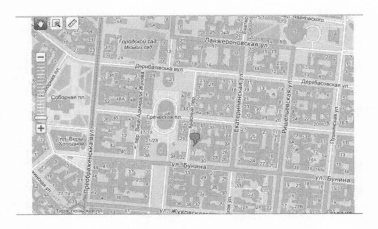

A map of the author's maternal
family home for over 145 years
Odessa Krasnuy Pereulok

Alla (left), Izya (middle)
and Mery (right)
Arkadia beach,
Odessa 1948

180

Alla (left), Dora (middle), Izya (right)
back row: little Danya (left) and little Bebbah
Odessa 1953

Danya
(David Izrailevich
Berdichevski)
Moscow–Red
Army, 1969

The Skulski family Dacha, Akerman
Emil Skulski (seated), Maga (left), Anushka
(right), and Alla Skulski (standing)
Odessa province 1962

Emil Skulski, fishing
at Turunchuk River
Odessa
province 1962

Emil and Alla Skulski
Sevastopol Crimea 1966

Alla (left), Maga (middle), Anushka
(right), summer cruise
Ivan Franko 1967
Beautiful Sochi—site of 2014 Winter Olympics

Emil playing with live bear, Goluboye Ozero
The Skulski family cruise to
Georgia, summer 1968

Alla and Izya, cruise on Ivan Franco
Yalta, Crimea 1968

Anushka (left), Maga (right)
Cruise on Ivan Franko
Crimea and Caucasus, summer 1969

Emil and Alla Skulski
Cruise on Ivan Franco, celebrating
New Year's party, 1970

185

Emil Skulski
(second from left)
Kippur War,
Sinai 1973

Meir Davidovich Skulski ({Zeida} far right)
Zionist Organization of Odessa, , Odessa 1925

Polya (left), little Karlusha ({Karl Skulski}
middle), Meir Davidovich Skuslki
(right) and little Miya Skulski
Odessa 1936

Karl Skulski (Karlusha), Masha (Dr. Mariya
Somoylovna Tikh), and Miya Skulski
Odessa 1935

Karl Skulski (upper left) with
fellow Fighter Pilots
German-occupied Nalchik,
North Caucasus, WWII 1941

Last photo of Meir Davidovich Skulski, Odessa 1970

A poem by Yohanan
Giterman written in Hebrew,
Dedicated to Meir
Davidovich Skulski (Zeida)
"Once There was a Nice
Man", Jerusalem 1975

An article dedicated to Meir
Davidovich Skulski, (Zeida)
Published in Jerusalem
newspaper, *Our Land* 1976

Maga (left) and Anushka Skulski
Odessa, Ukraine 1968

Alla (left) and Maga (middle)
visiting Anushka (right)
NYC, 1993

Emil Skulski, last photo taken in
Odessa before arrival in Israel, 1971

ACKNOWLEDGEMENTS

Thanks for reading my letters, which were written with much joy, although they also served to excavate some difficult memories and occasionally brought to the surface not-so-joyful recollections.

Many dark secrets surrounded my family, my father's death among them. But having said that, I did not wish to make this a dark book, but a loving tribute to the people I have been privileged to know.

Haa, the book.... I kept hopping and skipping from this and to that. No wonder it took nine years of nurturing and an occasional light bulb of inspiration for me to write this book to you, one letter at a time. While I did not write every day, nevertheless there were days when I could not stop writing, when I would fill up pages with events from over fifty years ago, thinking I may be writing my last letter, but eventually ending up with so many letters. Still ticking, I decided to compile those letters into this book. "I may as well," as Zeida used to say.

I owe it all to my amazing mother, who shared her cherished memories with me, never losing faith in my strength to overcome any obstacle that may keep me from writing. This book also would never have come to life without my Aunt Miya and my lovely niece Maga, who provided many family photos, articles and poems. And surely this book was doomed to keep collecting dust in my storage box if not for my editor, brilliant dear Karen Carter, who always "knew" with heart what I really meant to say, despite the way I sometimes say things and misplace words, and Jaye Manus, my very talented ebook designer and formatting specialist.

I give endless thanks to the JewishGen.org Odessa KehilaLink site for publishing an article about my Zeida, with a special appreciation to Ariel Parkansky for his kind assistance to me, a total stranger.

I also thank Helen Rock, an administrator at the Cancer Center at Nyack Hospital; Natalie Frier and Ulla Novina, rock sculptors; Veronica Dalcero and Dr. Michael Wesson from the Radiation Oncology department at the Valley Blumenthal Cancer Center; Donna Culnen from the Hackensack Radiology Group; Tennis For Life (TFL) of Bergen County; Bergen County Harley-Davidson/BMW; Amazon Heart; Lisa "Blue" Williams; Gilda's Club; Susan G. Komen for the Cure, Hawaii; EIF Revlon Run/Walk For Women; Veria Cable TV; Agora Gallery in New York; Chantal Lagross; Queens Museum of Art; JewishGen; National Library of Israel in Jerusalem; and Keren Kayemet LeIsrael-Jewish National Fund.

But beyond it all, I owe my thanks to people alongside whom I have been privileged to walk, and whose tender souls have kept my own alive, long after they were all gone. Still they keep guiding, inspiring and shielding. How else did I come to have the words and strength during all the years I kept writing the letters that evolved into the book you have just read?

AUTHOR'S NOTE

This book was scheduled to be published in October 2013 on my birthday and during my ninth year celebrating Life free of cancer. But due to an accident that involved a broken leg, the publication of this book was delayed. Little did I know I would eventually publish it while the world watched in horror as Ukraine became the innocent target of modern Russian aggression.

Sadly the current tragic events in Ukraine once again prove the Kremlin is not yet ready to let go, despite the Perestroika policies of the 1980s promoted by Mikhail Gorbachev, who was a true visionary and a wise man. Putin's regime is based on the old Communist philosophy of power and control. It is consumed with the fear of letting go and is incapable of coexisting with neighboring states. The saddest and most tragic part of all this is the harm it is doing to the people of Ukraine. Putin thinks of such suffering and the potential destruction of the beautiful land of Ukraine, the most fertile land of the former Soviet Union, as only collateral damage. But the people of Ukraine are proud, humble and hard-working individuals who will never give up. Sooner or later they will gain their land back from the iron fist of the Kremlin.

In the hope that such upheaval will soon die down in this region I am planning to undertake, in the nearby country of Georgia, a new challenge in order to reinvent myself yet again: climbing to the remote Caucasus Mountains valley of Tusheti, a hidden Shangri-La, to celebrate Life.

A.A.

Made in the USA
Charleston, SC
31 May 2014